the handbook guide to

Murder!

London Horror!

D1452090

From historic monuments
to private homes, sites of torture,
fear, death and execution

First published in 1998 by Handbook Publishing Ltd,
14 Anhalt Road, London SW11 4NX

ISBN 1-901309-04-5

Printed in England by Biddles Ltd, Guildford & Kings Lynn

Book and cover design by Ivan Bulloch
Maps compiled from the 1939 John Bartholomew Atlas revised from copyright-free aerial photography and checked on foot. Drawn and produced by Landfall Mapping, Southampton: tel. (01703) 730009/576187.

Cover illustrations © Mary Evans Picture Library.

Photographs © Crail Low, except: p4-5, 8-9, 23, 40, 56-57, 60 © Mary Evans Picture Library; p26-27 & 44-45 © Guildhall Library; p66-67 & 70 © Mirror Newspapers; p74 & 75 © British Library; p79 © Getty Images; p84-85 © Mail Newspapers; and p90-91 © Imperial War Museum.

Other titles
Rock & Pop London
Royal Life: town & country
The Thames: from source to sea

Contents

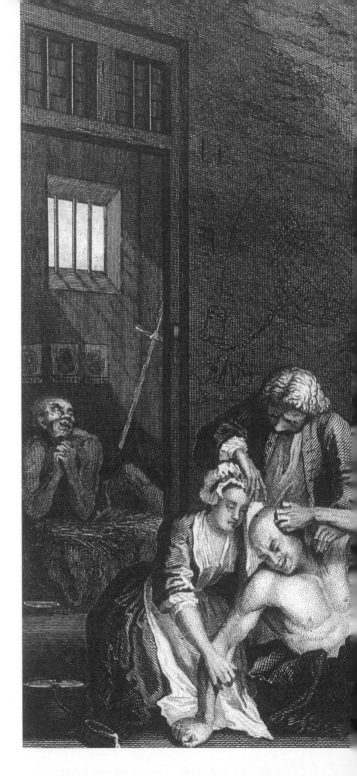

BEDLAM HOSPITAL FOR THE
INSANE AS DEPICTED BY
WILLIAM HOGARTH IN HIS
SERIES *THE RAKE'S PROGRESS*

Introduction

Today London is being reinvented as a city for the twenty-first century with the best of its two thousand years collected together for the future.

But what of the worst? What are the dark acts of the past that remind us of the dark side of human nature, which by remembering we may keep searching for a better tomorrow? Is it safe to forget the centuries of pestilence, pain and death? Should they not serve as a warning?

For many centuries, justice was rarely fair or even; punishment was mostly brutal, inappropriate or excessive. But so were the conditions of the time. Plagues, famines and violence saw to what hard work, malnutrition and lack of hygiene did not. Life for the majority, until not long ago, was brutal, painful and short.

Crime went largely unchecked: thieving, burglary and piracy were careers, with established guilds akin to more lawful professions.

Murder! Horror! London sets out to show the real city beneath the veneer of sophistication. For many of today's greatest monuments were built for very different, and more sinister, purposes: from the burning of witches at Smithfield Market to the Tyburn gallows at Marble Arch, from the chaining of pirates beneath the Thames at Wapping to the severed heads of criminals that greeted visitors at the gates to London.

With maps, visiting details, history and vivid illustrations, we show the darker side of London: where murderers carried out their horrific crimes, where gangsters ran their empires, where justice was given and sentences carried out.

Murder! Horror! London is not a guide to the macabre. It does not horrify with gory details. But rather it shows the darker aspects of London's history that have affected today's landscape.

For two thousand years, London has been a great city, but for at least as long it has been a violent one. Its dark past serves as a warning to the future.

A HANGING AT TYBURN BY WILLIAM HOGARTH

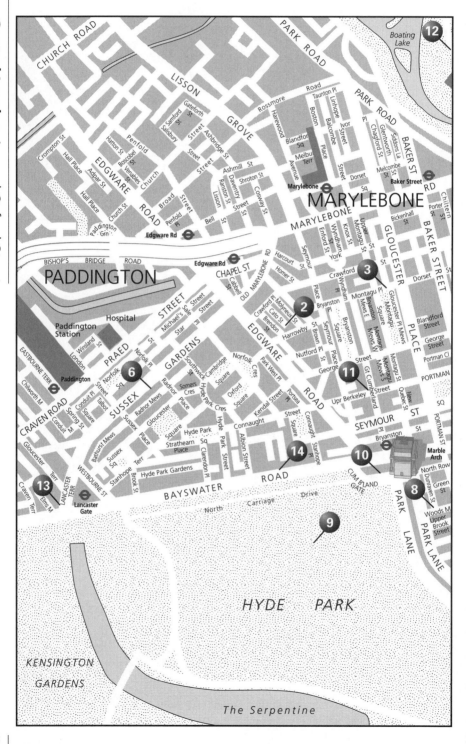

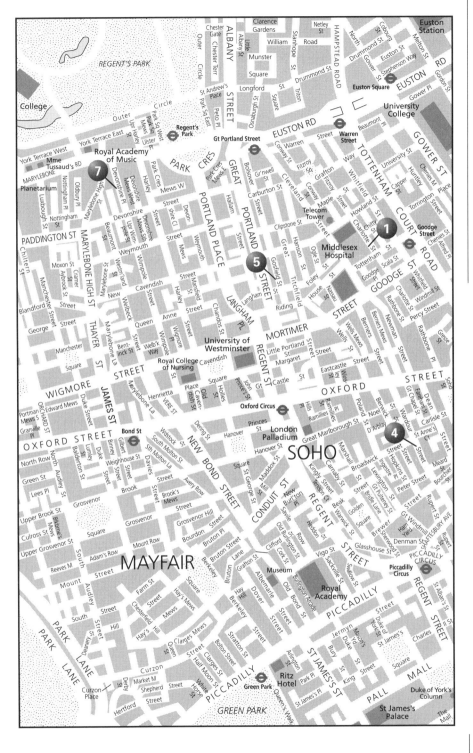

Central London

Around Oxford Street

Bayswater, Soho, Mayfair and Regent's Park

For nine centuries, hundreds of the country's most dangerous criminals were led to their execution on the site of today's Marble Arch.

In those days London as we know it was a series of villages divided by farms, great estates and woods. Villages like Bayswater, where highwaymen preyed on travellers journeying towards Oxford. Or parks like Regent's Park where royalty walked with their mistresses and were spied upon by their enemies.

The route to execution followed today's Oxford Street, passing the crime-infested streets of Soho where the maze of alleys and lanes had always lent themselves to the darker side of London life: pick-pocketing, prostitution and gang-led crime.

Some would look regretfully at the aristocratic houses in Mayfair where they had so frequently visited to burgle and kill.

Others would look wistfully across to Hyde Park where the dark trees and bushes had hid them in their care-free days of highway robbery.

And on each of these occasions, Oxford Street was as bustling then as it is today.

1| **Astor College** Charlotte Street W1

During the First World War, air raids provided a convenient cover for crime. Particularly notorious was that of the murder of Emilienne Gerard.

She was a Belgian woman separated from her husband, a French Army chef, and living in London. On 31 October 1917 there was a Zeppelin bombing raid and she fled with the crowds into a tube station to shelter. It was the last time she was seen alive.

Two days later, a road sweeper found a sheet containing her headless body in Regent Square. Nearby another parcel was discovered containing her legs. She was identified from the sheet's laundry mark.

The police went to inform her lover, Louis Voisin, a butcher living in the basement flat of 101 Charlotte Street.

On arriving, they were surprised to see Voisin in the arms of another woman, Berthe Roche. However, on examining the flat, they were more surprised to find not only the kitchen covered in human blood but Gerard's head in the outbuilding.

Voisin was charged with her murder and hanged at Pentonville.

Astor College, part of Middlesex Hospital, now stands on the site of 101 Charlotte Street.

2| **1A Cato Street** W1

The early nineteenth century was a time of political turbulence. The revolutions in Europe, particularly the French, continued to reverberate.

On 23 February 1820, a group of men met in the stable loft at this address to plot the assassination of the entire cabinet of government ministers as they dined at 44 Grosvenor Square that evening. The heads of several ministers, including the Home Secretary, were to be carried off in a bag. Afterwards mayhem was planned around the city.

However, one of the conspirators, George Edwards, had cold feet and informed the authorities. The Bow Street Runners (**see p.21**) stormed the stable loft, eventually arresting most of the group at the cost of one constable who was killed by Arthur Thistlewood, running him through with his sword. Eleven escaped but most were captured the following day.

The leaders were hanged outside Newgate Prison; the rest were transported. However, they had strong public support and the condemned men were spared being quartered. Indeed a few days later, the man suspected of hanging them was almost castrated by sympathetic crowds.

George Frederick Cummins
During 1942 a series of horrific sex crimes occurred that sent waves of panic through the streets of London as it was thought that another Jack the Ripper was on the loose.

Four bodies were found with their throats slashed and their bodies mutilated.

3| Montagu Place W1
Evelyn Hamilton, a school teacher, was found strangled in an air-raid shelter in Monatgu Place on 9 February, and her bag stolen.

4| 153 Wardour Street W1
On 10 February Nita Ward, an ex-actress, was killed at her flat on Soho's Wardour Street: her throat had been cut and her body mutilated with a tin-opener. Her handbag was also missing.

5| 9-10 Gosfield Street W1
The next day, 11 February, Margaret Lowe was found by her daughter, strangled with a stocking and her body cut by a razor, at her home in Gosfield Street.

6| 187 Sussex Gardens W2
The last body to be found was that of Doris Jouannet, a prostitute, at Sussex Gardens. She had also been strangled and cut with a razor.

The police were helpless and without clues until they investigated an assault on a woman in a Westminster pub. The assailant, a twenty-eight year old RAF cadet, George Frederick Cummins, was arrested and charged. The case merited only a couple of lines in the newspapers. But by chance, they were read by a Mrs Mulcahy who recognised Cummins as the man who had also attempted to assault her at her home at Southwick Street. After informing the police, his lodgings were searched and several ladies handbags found. They belonged to the women killed in February.

Cummins was hanged on 25 June 1942 for the murders.

HYDE PARK
ONCE THE HAUNT OF
HIGHWAYMEN

7│ 2 Devonshire Place W1

Here, the young Arthur Conan Doyle had an unsuccessful medical practice in the late 1880s. During the frequent gaps between patients, he idled his time with an idea for a scientific detective. This character became Sherlock Holmes, based at the fictional address of 221b Baker Street, NW1.

Sherlock Holmes became fabulously successful, solving his cases with a ruthless intellect. Many of the cases involved London, with its swirling fog, gas lamps and hansom cabs almost as characters in themselves. *The Sign of Four* used the grand Langham Hotel, Portland Place W1 and in *The Hounds of the Baskervilles*, Sir Henry Baskerville stays at the Strand in Northumberland Street, WC2. The hotel has been replaced by a pub, renamed the Sherlock Holmes and with a perfect reconstruction of his study upstairs.

8│ Dunraven Street (then 14 Norfolk Street) W1

One of the most sensational murder trials of the nineteenth century began on 6 May 1840 when the seventy year old Lord William Russell was discovered with his throat cut to the spine. Russell was one of the grandest men in the country. Brother of both the 5th and 6th Dukes of Bedford, he was also uncle to the cabinet minister, Lord John Russell.

He was a widower and lived simply with a staff of three. One of them a twenty-three year old Swiss valet, named Francois Courvoisier, the police immediately charged with the crime.

However they had no proof and when the case came to trial, it was widely thought that he would be acquitted. Only on the last day, before the jury retired, did a chance sequence of events change matters. The husband of an ex-employer of Courvoisier was reading the newspaper and mentioned the case to his wife. This reminded her that Courvoisier had recently sent her a parcel for safekeeping. Not knowing what to do, she sent the parcel to the police. They opened it and discovered silver stolen from Russell's house. It was the hard evidence required and on 6 July 1840 Courvoisier was hanged in front of a hundred thousand spectators at Newgate. Russell's house has since been rebuilt.

9| Hyde Park

Since its creation by Henry VIII from church land, the royal park has had a long association with crime. The trees and bushes provided good camouflage for highwaymen to prey on wealthy travellers passing through. Indeed so bad and frequent did the attacks become that a squad of mounted policemen were formed.

The large secluded spaces of the park also provided ideal locations for affairs of honour to be settled by duelling. Using either pistols or swords, rarely a week would pass without gallants facing each other, promising to go to the death to defend their good name. More often than not, the duels were settled without injury or blood spilt. However many were not. In 1712, Lord Mohun and the Duke of Hamilton's first onslaught was so violent that Mohun was killed outright and Hamilton minutes later.

In 1816 Harriet Westbrook drowned herself in the Serpentine Lake. She was the wife of Percy Bysshe Shelley and had been distraught that the poet had run off with his soon to be second wife, Mary (author of *Frankenstein*, **see p.71**).

The most recent horror witnessed by Hyde Park was on 20 July 1982 when a car-bomb exploded on South Carriage Drive. Two horse-guards, on their way to the Changing of the Guards, were killed and seventeen spectators injured. The IRA claimed responsibility for this and a similar bomb that exploded two hours later in Regent's Park (**see no.12**).

10| Marble Arch W1

Marble Arch was the location of the Tyburn gallows, the most famous execution site in London. Over fifty thousand met their death here between the twelfth century and 1783, when the gallows were moved to Newgate Prison in the City.

In 1571, the first permanent gallows in London were erected here and named the Tyburn Tree after the local river, now underground. The gallows were triangular in shape, eighteen feet high and could hang up to twenty-four people at the same time.

Executions were public and, though intended as a deterrent to crime, became great spectacles, with the victims often seen as heroes. Indeed, many believed that the touch of a hanged man would cure illnesses. Tens of thousands would descend on Tyburn on execution day which was also made a public holiday, known as a 'hanging match' or a 'Tyburn Fair'. Over two hundred thousand came to watch Jack Sheppard (**see p.36**) hang in 1724, with thousands paying to visit him in his Newgate cell prior to his death.

The condemned prisoners were brought to Tyburn from Newgate Prison in a cart, along with their coffin. (The slang for execution was 'going West'.) So crowded were the streets that the journey could take up to two hours, with frequent stops for 'last drinks' en route so the victim often arrived drunk. If the condemned was unpopular, they would be pelted with missiles. For example, the murderess Elizabeth Brownrigg (**see p.34**) had dead rats and stones thrown at her on the journey to Tyburn.

When the cart arrived at the gallows, a rope was attached to the victim's neck and the horse whipped to move away, leaving the victim dangling.

EXECUTION

THE FIRST RECORDED EXECUTION IN ENGLAND WAS THAT OF THE EARL OF HUNTINGDON IN 1076. THE LAST WAS IN AUGUST 1964 AND CAPITAL PUNISHMENT WAS ABOLISHED FOR A TRIAL PERIOD IN 1965.

OFTEN CRIMINALS WERE GIBBETED AFTER EXECUTION: THE BODIES WERE HUNG FROM CHAINS AFTER DEATH AS A WARNING TO OTHERS. (GIBBETING WAS ABOLISHED IN 1834.)

PLACES OF EXECUTION WERE COMMONLY LOCATED ON ROUTES INTO LONDON TO SERVE AS DETERRENTS. THE SIGHT OF DEAD BODIES HANGING AND ROTTING AFTER DEATH WERE INTENDED TO WARD OFF POSSIBLE CRIMINALS.

THE DEATH PENALTY

TREASON AND VIOLENT CRIME WERE PUNISHABLE BY EITHER BEHEADING OR HANGING. WITCHES WERE BURNT AT THE STAKE AND POISONERS WERE BOILED ALIVE. BY THE SEVENTEENTH CENTURY, THE NUMBER OF CRIMES PUNISHABLE BY DEATH ROSE FROM FIFTEEN TO FIFTY.

DURING JUST TEN YEARS OF THE REIGN OF JAMES I IN THE EARLY SEVENTEENTH CENTURY NEARLY ONE THOUSAND FIVE HUNDRED WERE EXECUTED IN LONDON AND MIDDLESEX.

Most deaths were caused by strangulation, with bodies convulsing for up to forty minutes (known as 'dancing the Paddington Frisk'). The clothes and the rope were later sold by the hangman. If the victims were lucky, friends would come forward and hold down their legs, or beat their hearts, to speed death. Sometimes, indeed, the victim's body would be supported in the hope of receiving a late reprieve. An example was John 'Half Hanged' Smith in 1709, who received his pardon and survived after being hanged.

An earlier example was in 1447 when five men were sentenced to be hanged, drawn and quartered. Just alive, they were cut down and stripped ready for quartering when their pardons arrived. But though now free men, the hangmen refused to return their clothes and they were forced to walk home naked.

After death, the victims were buried nearby, or sold to hospitals for experiment. Hangings did not always go to plan, for example several like the thief John Haynes in 1772, though declared dead, regained consciousness on the dissection table. Of course there would be no reprieve and they would be returned to Tyburn.

The last execution to take place at Tyburn was that of John Austin, a robber, in 1783.

11 | The Masons Arms 51 Upper Berkeley Street W1

The cellar of the pub was created from dungeons that held those awaiting execution at Tyburn. The victims were supposedly led to their hanging via a tunnel from the pub.

12 | Regent's Park NW1

During one of the many periods of IRA violence in London, Regent's Park was targeted when, on the hot afternoon of 20 July 1982, a bomb exploded under the bandstand beside the lake. Six bands-men of the Royal Green Jackets Regiment were killed and many spectators injured.

Two hours earlier a similar bomb had exploded in Hyde Park (**see no.9**).

THE SWAN (TOP RIGHT)
LAST DRINKING PLACE FOR
LONDON'S CONDEMNED

REGENT'S PARK BANDSTAND
REBUILT IN MEMORY OF THOSE
WHO WERE KILLED

13| The Swan 66 Bayswater Road W2
This popular inn was frequented by criminals having a traditional last drink before reaching the Tyburn gallows.

14| Tyburn Convent 8 Hyde Park Place, Bayswater Road W2
Tel. 0171-723 7262
Tours of shrine: daily 10am, 3.30pm & 5.30pm
Chapel open daily 6.30am-8.30pm for prayer
Free
The Tyburn Convent is the home of French Benedictine nuns. In the basement is a shrine to the Catholic martyrs executed at Tyburn during the years of the Reformation. A reconstruction of the gallows stands over the altar.

The first Catholic to be executed at Tyburn was John Houghton in 1535, the Prior of the Carthusian monastery at Charterhouse (**see p.32**); and the last was Oliver Plunket, the Primate of Ireland who was accused of taking part in the Popish Plot of 1681.

CRIMES PUNISHED BY DEATH
IN THE FOLLOWING CENTURIES, MORE AND MORE CRIMES WERE GIVEN THE DEATH SENTENCE. 1810 WAS THE WATERMARK WITH TWO HUNDRED AND TWENTY-TWO CRIMES PUNISHABLE BY DEATH, INCLUDING: FORGERY, ARSON, RAPE, SODOMY, PIRACY, DESTROYING OR BURNING SHIPS, BANKRUPTS HIDING ASSETS; BURGLARY, HIGHWAY ROBBERY, HOUSE-BREAKING, PICK-POCKETING ABOVE ONE SHILLING, SHOPLIFTING ABOVE FIVE SHILLINGS, STEALING ABOVE FORTY SHILLINGS; SHOOTING AT A REVENUE OFFICER, PULLING DOWN BUILDINGS, DESTROYING A POND CONTAINING FISH; CUTTING DOWN TREES, HOPS, OR VEGETATION ON RIVER OR SEA BANKS, SETTING FIRE TO CORN OR COAL MINES; RETURN FROM TRANSPORTATION, STABBING AN UNARMED VICTIM WHO DIES WITHIN SIX MONTHS, CONCEALING THE DEATH OF AN ILLEGITIMATE CHILD; MALICIOUS MAIMING; THE SENDING OF THREATENING LETTERS; RIOTS BY TWELVE OR MORE PEOPLE AND NOT DISPERSING AN HOUR AFTER THE MAGISTRATE'S PROCLAMATION; BEING AN ACCESSORY TO A CAPITAL FELONY; STEALING ANIMALS; ESCAPE FROM PRISON; SACRILEGE, SMUGGLING, MAIL ROBBERY, DESTRUCTION OF BRIDGES OR TURNPIKES; IMPERSONATING A CHELSEA PENSIONER.

THE SITUATION WAS RIDICULOUS AND IN 1861 ONLY FOUR REMAINED: MURDER, TREASON, ARSON IN A ROYAL DOCKYARD AND PIRACY.

ST MARTIN-IN-THE-FIELDS AS SEEN ACROSS TRAFALGAR SQUARE

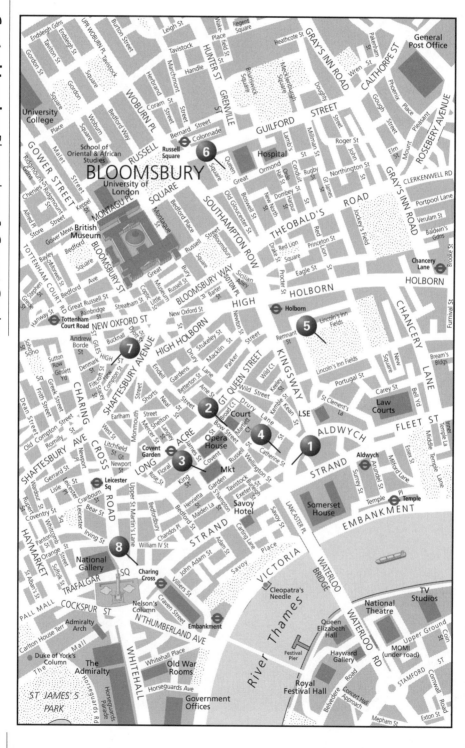

Bloomsbury & Covent Garden

Built in the early seventeenth century, Covent Garden has always been a place of entertainment, excitement, romance and … murder.

Until the roots of the police force were established in the district, violent gangs ruled and roamed the streets. Pimps and prostitutes, duels and crimes of passion were frequent scenes. Only around the time of the present Queen's Silver Jubilee in 1977 was Covent Garden resurrected as a centre of entertainment.

To the north, Bloomsbury was an area of simple fields until developed by the Russell family. And here tragically amidst their finest development they came to see the execution of their greatest member, beheaded for treason.

From the lowest to the highest, from the execution of a lord to the murder of a mistress, life was always close to death for those on the streets of central London.

1 | Aldwych WC2
On 18 February 1996, shortly after an IRA cease-fire had been abandoned, a bomb exploded on a bus travelling along Aldwych. Its detonation appeared to be premature as Edward O'Brien, a member of the IRA, died along with four of the bus's innocent passengers. He had been carrying the bomb.

It is likely that the explosive was being transported to the City. For only nine days before, a 225kg IRA bomb went off at South Quay, Canary Wharf in the Docklands. The bomb had killed two people, but had injured over a hundred and caused devastating damage to property.

The Canary Wharf explosion occurred just two minutes after the IRA called off their cease-fire at 6pm that evening.

2 | Bow Street Magistrates Court Bow Street WC2
Bow Street Magistrates Court has been here since the 1740s when Henry Fielding (author of *Tom Thumb* and *Tom Jones*) was a magistrate. To combat the organised and violent criminal gangs of the time, Fielding, and his blind half-brother John, the next magistrate, set about the establishment of a body of men to more effectively enforce the law.

They appointed seven 'thief-takers' known as 'Mr Fielding's People' and soon renamed their law-enforcers, the Bow Street Runners. Also established was a foot patrol servicing a radius of four miles around the City, and later in 1805 a horse patrol to police an even greater area.

The Bow Street Runners took over from the more informal predecessors and became the forerunners of the modern police force, lasting until 1839.

3 | Covent Garden Piazza WC2
One of the saddest crimes of passion took place on 7 April 1779 with the murder of Martha Ray. Only thirty years old, she was the mistress of the ageing Earl of Sandwich, by whom she had borne nine children. However she had a secret lover, James Hackman, an impoverished army officer who

EARLY HEALTH

THE EARLY CENTURIES WERE A PRECARIOUS TIME FOR THE HEALTH OF LONDON. CRAMPED CONDITIONS AND THE IGNORANCE OF DISEASE LED TO EPIDEMICS THAT DECIMATED THE POPULATION.

MEDICINE WAS LARGELY BASED ON SUPERSTITION AND FOLKLORE. THE CURES FOR MOST AILMENTS LAY IN A PRESCRIPTION OF HERBS AND THE LETTING OF UP TO A PINT OF THE PATIENT'S BLOOD. WHEN SCIENCE WAS USED, IT WAS CRUDE. FOR EXAMPLE, VENEREAL DISEASES WERE TREATED BY OFTEN FATAL DOSES OF MERCURY.

KNOWLEDGE OF PUBLIC HYGIENE WAS NEGLIGIBLE. UNTIL THE NINETEENTH CENTURY, THERE WERE NEVER MORE THAN FIFTEEN MILES OF SEWERAGE IN THE ENTIRE CITY. LAVATORIES WERE BUILT OVER RIVERS FROM WHICH DRINKING WATER WAS DRAWN. REFUSE OF ALL FORMS ROTTED IN THE STREETS, UNTIL WASHED AWAY BY RAIN. PERSONAL CLEANLINESS WAS LARGELY IGNORED AND HOUSES WERE RIDDLED WITH VERMIN, PARTICULARLY DANGEROUS BEING THE RATS CARRYING THE PLAGUE FLEA.

had recently become a priest to secure an income for their future together. But it was not enough: Martha did not wish to lose the security of the Earl and refused to see Hackman any more.

Hackman was distraught and stalked her until that fatal spring evening. As she descended the steps of the Royal Opera House, he shot her with one of two pistols. He then attempted to follow her in death but the pistol failed, leaving him to batter his head with the gun in desperation.

At his trial, Hackman evoked great sympathy and even the Earl of Sandwich appealed for mercy on his behalf. But he was determined to die and hanged at Tyburn.

4| Drury Lane Theatre Catherine Street WC2

Since its construction in the seventeenth century, Drury Lane Theatre has been frequented by royalty.

Nell Gwynne made her acting debut here in 1665, after progressing from selling oranges in nearby Covent Garden. Her success was such that King Charles II was intrigued to meet her and once they had met, she quickly became his mistress, bearing him several children.

In 1779, Mary Robinson was one of Thomas Gainsborough's most famous models and also a successful actress. After her stunning performance in *A Winter's Tale*, she was introduced to the Prince of Wales (the future King George IV) and became his mistress.

Twelve years later, his brother, the future William IV, saw the actress Mrs Jordan perform, before she became his mistress and bore him many children.

DRURY LANE THEATRE
A ROYAL FAVOURITE

But other royal visits to the Drury Lane Theatre have been less than pleasant. In 1716, the future George II attended a play and narrowly missed being shot by a man named Freeman. And then in 1800, George III was watching a play here when James Hadfield tried unsuccessfully to assassinate him. Hadfield was caught, declared insane and committed to Bedlam Hospital for life.

5| Lincoln's Inn Fields WC1

Before the square was developed, Lincoln's Inn Fields were common grazing land with an execution site on the present day bandstand.

During the religious turmoil of the sixteenth and seventeenth centuries many executions took place here, including in 1586, Anthony Babington and thirteen fellow Catholics who were hanged, drawn and quartered for plotting to murder Elizabeth I and replace her with the Catholic Mary, Queen of Scots.

In 1683, Lord William Russell, who lived in nearby Southampton Street, was executed for his part in the Rye House Plot, a failed conspiracy to assassinate Charles II and his Catholic brother, the future James II, at Rye House in Hertfordshire as they returned to London. The plot hoped to secure the succession of Charles' illegitimate and Protestant son, the Duke of Monmouth.

A DISSECTION AT THE ROYAL
COLLEGE OF SURGEONS
BY WILLIAM HOGARTH

Russell's father was awarded the Dukedom of Bedford in 1694 by the monarchs, William and Mary, as recognition for his son's sacrifice to the Protestant cause.

Nos. 59-60 were the home of Spencer Percival, the only Prime Minister to be assassinated (**see p.60**).

35 Lincoln's Inn Fields is home to the **Royal College of Surgeons**. The College was founded in 1540 as the Barber-Surgeon Company. The Company secured a charter to receive four bodies annually from Tyburn executions for dissection and the College still has the skeletons of several criminals.

The Hunterian Museum (not open to the general public) is housed in the building, containing thousands of anatomical specimens from the collection of the eighteenth century surgeon, John Hunter.

Bodies for anatomical dissection at the country's medical schools were at a premium in eighteenth century England. Anyone buried was under threat of being 'body-snatched'. Surgeons desperate for specimens encouraged the likes of Burke and Hare in Glasgow to steal bodies from graves. There were even cases of murders taking place specifically to sell the bodies for dissection. In London, Bishop and Williams hanged for such an offence.

6 | The Queen's Larder pub 1 Queen Square WC1

George III stayed at the nearby home of Dr Willis during his first bout of 'madness', caused by prophyria, a rare metabolic disorder.

The illness first struck the King in 1788 with symptoms that shocked the court: he was caught talking to a tree and even worse, attacked his son during a dinner at Windsor Castle. His treatments at Queen Square were often humiliating and horrific. George was tied down into an iron chair and disgusting remedies were smeared over his body.

QUEEN'S LARDER PUB
SECRET FOOD STORE FOR
GEORGE III

During the King's confinement at Queen Square, his wife, Queen Charlotte, stored delicacies for her husband in the cellar of this pub.

7| St Giles-in-the-Fields St Giles High Street WC2

The church was built on the site of a twelfth century leper hospital, dedicated to the patron saint of outcasts. During this time, leprosy was London's greatest health problem, more feared even than the plague.

In later centuries, when passing the church, prisoners travelling from Newgate to their execution at Tyburn were given 'cups of charity' at the gate.

In 1665 the Great Plague began in this parish and in the churchyard lie the stacked and often unnamed bodies of the plague's victims who lived in the area.

"Multitudes, multitudes, in the valley of the shadow of death throbbing daily into Eternity." DR VINCENT, 1665

Also buried here are five Catholics, executed for their part in the Popish Plot of 1681 to murder Charles II. They included Oliver Plunket, the Archbishop of Armagh.

8| St Martin-in-the-Fields St Martin's Place, Trafalgar Square WC2

In the graveyard lies buried Charles II's favourite mistress, Nell Gwynne (died 1687) and the notorious thief, Jack Sheppard. His daring (escaping from Newgate Prison four times) made him a very popular villain and after his execution at Tyburn in 1724, the crowd buried him here, having prevented surgeons taking the body for dissection.

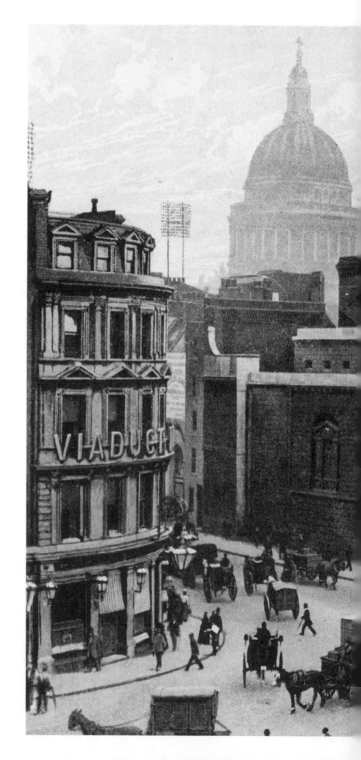

NEWGATE PRISON

PHOTOGRAPHED PRIOR TO ITS

DEMOLITION IN 1902

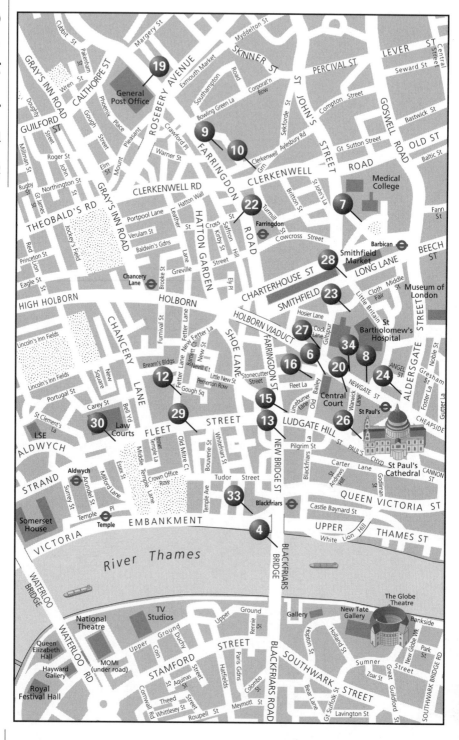

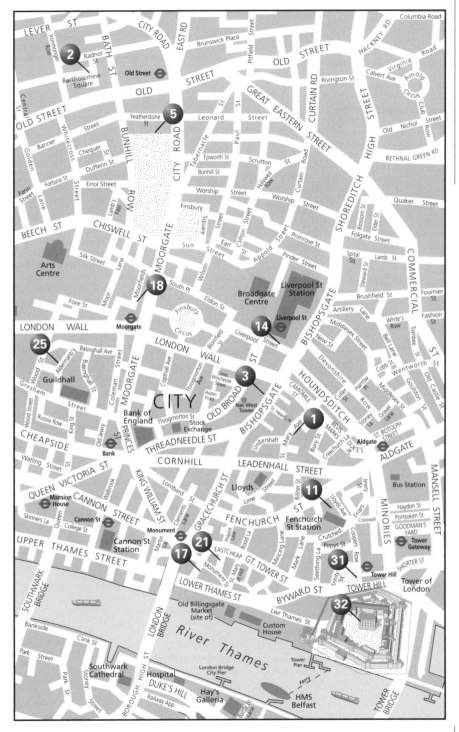

The City

The City is the ancient heart of London. From here the greatest wealth emanates. Outside its walls, however, stand some of the poorest and most violent communities. The City survives despite the many attacks to its existence, from revolts of a thousand years ago to terrorist bombs during the last decade.

In the City, crime and punishment existed in their most powerful forms: the boiling of witches at Smithfield Market, the hung, drawn and quartered traitors at the Tower of London and the torturing at Newgate where prisoners were left to rot.

Nobody ever said they didn't deserve it, from pirates and regicides to cut-throat murderers. And until just over a hundred years ago, at least two hundred crimes were capital offences.

1| Baltic Exchange St Mary Axe EC3

On 10 April 1992, days after the general election which saw John Major and the Conservatives re-elected to power, the Baltic Exchange was severely damaged by an IRA bomb. Three people were killed.

2| Bartholomew Square EC1

At the start of 1903, George Chapman appeared a hard-working publican and grieving widower of three wives. However nothing was as it seemed. For a start his real name was Severin Klosowski, secondly he moved pubs frequently as each enterprise failed and thirdly, each new wife had died suddenly.

Chapman began at the Prince of Wales pub on Bartholomew Square, with his wife, Mary Spink. Her death on Christmas Day 1898 passed without suspicion. Within weeks he had advertised and recruited a barmaid, Bessie Taylor, who soon became his second wife. They moved to the Monument Tavern on Union Street, SE1, where she too died. Her death again passed without suspicion. Apparently inconsolable, he proposed to Maud Marsh, another pretty barmaid, and again moved pubs to The Crown at 213 Borough High Street, SE1. Her parents did not approve of, or like, Chapman and when, inevitably, their daughter died, they insisted upon a private autopsy. Their suspicions were confirmed: she had been poisoned.

A full investigation followed. The bodies of Chapman's two former wives were exhumed and found to have been poisoned. No motive for the murders could be found other than Chapman's need to bully and brutalise women. Chapman was charged and hanged at Wandsworth prison in April 1903.

3| Bishopsgate EC2

Entry to the City of London is as protected now as it was in Roman times when a wall was built to keep out hostile forces. The recent police presence (known as 'the ring of steel') was created to prevent such acts of terrorism as the bomb which exploded on 24 April 1993.

The IRA, in one of their frequent mainland forays, had planted a bomb in a van parked here, on the corner of Bishopsgate and Wormwood Street.

The explosion shook the City of London, killing one man and injuring fifty, with damage totalling over £1 billion.

4| Blackfriars Bridge EC4

On 15 June 1982 the body of Roberto Calvi was found hanging beneath the arches of the bridge. Calvi, an Italian banker, was deeply involved with the Vatican in fraudulent business loans which led to the collapse of his bank, Banco Ambrosiano. He had fled to England, he thought secretly, carrying only a suitcase filled with money.

Although his killers were never found, it is thought that displaying his body in such a prominent place was a warning to others involved in the fraud not to aid any investigation.

Several years later, on the night of 20 August 1989, two hundred young people were celebrating a twenty-first birthday aboard the small pleasure boat, the Marchioness. They came from the glamorous worlds of media, fashion and society. As they danced, their boat was hit. Just by Blackfriars Bridge, the two thousand ton dredger, Bowbell, rammed the Marchioness from behind and it sunk immediately, causing the deaths of over fifty-seven passengers.

5| Bunhill Fields City Road EC1

Originally intended as a burial ground for plague victims, the land was used from the seventeenth to nineteenth centuries as a city graveyard. The lack of space here, and elsewhere in central London, led to the creation of larger suburban cemeteries.

6| Central Criminal Court Old Bailey EC4

Tel. 0171-248 3277
Open Mon-Fri 10am-4.30pm (no children under 14)
Free

First built in 1539 beside the old Newgate Prison (**see no.20**), the present building houses nineteen court rooms used for criminal trials and seventy cells. The entrance to the court was the debtor's door to the prison and it was outside here that public executions took place.

Of the hundreds of famous trials held at the Old Bailey were those of Oscar Wilde for homosexuality (1895), Crippen for wife-murder (1910), George Joseph Smith, the Brides in the Bath murderer (1915), Christie, the serial murderer (1953), the Krays for gangland killings (1968) and Peter Sutcliffe, the Yorkshire Ripper (1981).

Traditionally a prisoner condemned to death would be given his sentence standing in front of a judge wearing a black cloth upon his wig. Those condemned of treason would hear the sentence spoken, "You shall be hanged up by the neck, but cut down alive, your entrails cut off from your body, and burned in your sight, your head to be severed from your body and your body divided into four parts and disposed of at the King's pleasure."

THE OLD BAILEY
LONDON'S CENTRAL CRIMINAL
COURT

7| Charterhouse Charterhouse Square EC1
Tel. 0171-253 9503
Guided tours Apr-July: Wed 2.15pm
Admission charge
The site of Charterhouse was originally a plague pit for victims of the fourteenth century Black Death. At its height, over two hundred bodies were buried here daily. Soon after the medieval epidemic a monastery was built on the land. The events of the next two centuries made some believe that the land was cursed.

During the Reformation, many of the monks from the monastery refused to swear allegiance to the new head of the church, Henry VIII, and as a consequence were executed.

In 1547, Charterhouse was given over to the Duke of Northumberland. But the new owner had little good fortune. After the death of Henry VIII's heir, Edward VI, Northumberland tried to place his daughter-in-law, Lady Jane Grey, on the throne at the expense of Henry's daughter Mary I. The attempt failed and he was promptly executed.

The following owner the Duke of Norfolk, who acquired the property in 1565, was executed by Elizabeth I for supporting the Catholic Mary Queen of Scots in 1572.

8| Christ Church Newgate Street EC1
Only the spire remains of Wren's church destroyed during the Blitz, where prisoners from Newgate Prison were buried.

Among those buried here include Queen Isabella in 1358 who had murdered her estranged husband Edward II, the author Thomas Malory in

1471 during imprisonment for treason, and Elizabeth Barton, the Holy Maid of Kent, who in 1534 tried to persuade Henry VIII not to divorce Catherine of Aragon and was consequently executed for treason.

9| Clerkenwell House of Detention Clerkenwell Close EC1
Tel. 0171-253 9494
Open daily 10am-6pm
Admission charge
The detention house was built in 1616 as an overflow for Newgate Prison (**see no.20**). It was situated next to the Clerkenwell overflow for Bridewell Prison (**see no.33**) built in 1615. They both closed in 1877 and were demolished in 1890.

Today a private museum is based in the network of subterranean cells. Here prison life and conditions are evoked in the dark, damp, cold and grim environment.

10| Clerkenwell Green EC1
During the nineteenth century the area was a centre for the disposal of stolen goods. Based here was Ikey Solomon, perhaps the most powerful 'fence' of his day, who, until his fall, had a vast network of thieves working for him.

Charles Dickens knew the area well from his days as a journalist and used it in *Oliver Twist* when Oliver was introduced to crime by the Artful Dodger and Fagin, a thinly disguised portrait of Solomon.

11| Fenchurch Street Station Railway Place EC3
On 9 July 1864 Thomas Briggs left Fenchurch Street Station to travel home to Hackney. As a chief bank clerk, he settled comfortably into his first class carriage.

However on arrival at Hackney, boarding passengers discovered blood and a hat in the empty carriage. A search was instigated and after several hours, Briggs was found dying on the tracks near Bow. The police had nothing to go on but the hat found in the carriage. Luckily it was a

CHARTERHOUSE
BUILT ON THE SITE OF A BURIAL
PIT FOR PLAGUE VICTIMS

particular type of flattened hat and they were able to trace it to a German tailor, Franz Muller.

But Muller had fled the country by sailing ship for America. The police took a faster steam ship and arrived in New York days before the German. The news made headlines, so that when Muller eventually docked, he was greeted by the police as the large crowd shouted "Welcome Muller, the German killer".

The death of Thomas Briggs was Britain's first railway murder.

12 | Fetter Lane EC4

This street has long been associated with crime and punishment as Fetter Lane was used frequently as a place of execution.

At the Fleet Street end, Sarah Malcolm was hanged in 1733 for the murder of a Mrs Duncomb and her two maidservants. At her trial, Sarah was viewed as a particularly tragic figure. An attractive, educated woman of twenty-two, she had been forced to work laundering clothes after her father had gambled away the family fortune.

The temptation of Mrs Duncomb's wealth had been too much. Upon her arrest Sarah was found to have the enormous sum of £53 hidden in her hair.

Two days before her execution, William Hogarth paid Sarah £5 to paint her portrait.

Opposite Fleur de Lis Court lived the murderess Elizabeth Brownrigg. Brownrigg, the mother of sixteen children, set up a lying-in hospital for pregnant women at her house. For staff she recruited orphan girls from the nearby workhouse at St Dunstan's-in-the-West. At first things went normally, but then something snapped in Brownrigg and she became a monster.

The girls were treated like slaves. Vicious punishment and ill-treatment became commonplace. As time went on Brownrigg placed the girls in the coal cellar, where they were kept chained by the neck and suspended from the beams, starved and flogged to the point of collapse.

Only when a neighbour heard the screams did the authorities investigate and found two girls barely alive and one, Mary Clifford, dead.

Brownrigg was hanged on 14 September 1767 at Tyburn and her body was given to the Royal College of Surgeons for dissection.

13 | Fleet Prison Ludgate Hill EC4

The prison was first built in Norman times on the east bank of the Fleet River. At its height it never covered more than an acre of ground and was surrounded by a moat. Though some debtors were held here, most were convicted by the Crown.

Torture and punishment were commonplace, including the pillory, branding, mutilation, thumbscrews and iron collars to suffocate prisoners. Torture took place in the dungeon, known as the 'Strong Room'. In 1846 the prison was demolished and a railway built on the land.

During the eighteenth and early nineteenth centuries, 'Fleet Marriages' took place when those in need of a quick and discrete ceremony used the

History of Prisons

Before prisons were widespread, punishment was carried out swiftly either in the form of a fine or as punishment by death or mutilation. Prison was used only for holding those awaiting trial or execution, and debtors.

It was the church who introduced the idea of using confinement as a punishment in itself. This began in the ninth century when they would imprison wayward clerics who had failed to abide by church law.

Only in the eighteenth century did prison become used as a punishment for society in general. With the greater wealth brought by the Industrial Revolution, new, large and more modern prisons, suitable for sentences of confinement, were able to be built.

services of priests held in the prison for debt. One such marriage was that of Maria Fitzherbert to the Prince of Wales, later George IV, on 5 September 1745. Their bankrupted priest was paid £500 and promised a bishopric.

The eighteenth century artist William Hogarth was very familiar with the prison as his father had been held there for debt in his early years. He portrayed the prison in several of his works, including, most famously, *The Rake's Progress*, where the 'hero' squanders his father's money and ends up in the Fleet for debt. The last image in the series, is that of Bedlam Hospital (**see no.18**) where he spends his last few years.

14| **Liverpool Street Station** EC2

The railway station was the site of Bethlehem Hospital from 1329 to 1674 (**see no.18**) and also of a large seventeenth century plague pit.

One inmate of the lunatic hospital, a giant named Daniel, was over seven feet tall. He had been a porter to Oliver Cromwell and started preaching through the bars of the asylum after Nell Gwynne gave him a bible. On forecasting the Great Fire of London, his fame grew with large crowds coming to hear him.

15| **Ludgate Prison** Ludgate Hill EC4

Ludgate Prison stands on the site of the original Lud Gate which was the Roman entrance to their burial site on the present day Fleet Street.

Ludgate was a medieval prison for petty criminals and debtors. One inmate was Stephen Forster, imprisoned as a boy for debt. Luckily fortune shone on Forster when a wealthy widow saw him through a window and liking him, paid his debts. She took him to live in her house and within just a few years they had married. In 1454, Forster became Lord Mayor of London.

16| **The Magpie & Stump** 18 Old Bailey EC4

The pub stands opposite the Old Bailey. When the courts were the site of Newgate Prison, the upper rooms were let out to spectators to view the public hangings which took place outside from 1783 to 1868.

17| **Monument** Monument Street EC3

Tel. 0171-626 2717
Open Mon-Fri 9am-6pm & w/e 2-6pm (Nov-Mar: Mon-Sat 9am-4pm)
Admission charge

The column was built by Christopher Wren in 1671 to commemorate the Great Fire of 1666. Though it destroyed over thirteen thousand houses, the fire killed only nine people.

The height of the column, two hundred and two feet, marks the distance to where the fire began in Pudding Lane (**see no.21**). Before 1842, when the gallery at the top of the monument was caged in, at least six people had jumped to their death.

18| **Moorfields** EC2

Originally open space by one of the entry gates to London, Moorfields was, during the seventeenth century, notorious for prostitution and crime.

Indeed it was nicknamed 'Sodomites Walk' because of the male prostitutes who frequently blackmailed their customers.

In 1674, Bethlehem Lunatic Asylum moved to Moorfields from the Liverpool Street Station area (**see no.14**) until the hospital was transferred to Lambeth (**see p.50**) in 1815.

The hospital was popular with visitors who paid to view the inmates, some of whom were kept in irons for many years. (**See picture p.4-5.**)

19│ Mount Pleasant Post Office Farringdon Road EC1
This was the site of Cold Bath Fields Prison between 1794 and 1889, well-known for its harsh conditions as described by Coleridge and Southey in *The Devil's Thoughts*:

"As he went through Coldbath Fields, he saw a solitary cell;
and the Devil was pleased,
for it gave him a hint for improving his prisons in hell."

20│ Newgate Prison Newgate Street EC1
Built in the twelfth century as the county gaol for London and Middlesex, Newgate's conditions were always notoriously bad. A mixture of contaminated water and a suffocating lack of ventilation led to almost incessant bouts of 'Gaol Fever', a vicious form of typhoid. Indeed, it was common for prisoners to be bathed in vinegar before attending court to mask their stench and for members of the judiciary to work behind nosegays of scented herbs.

Torture was commonplace and confessions were obtained by placing heavy weights on the body in the Pressing Yard. Also 'pressed' were those who refused to plead to a charge, often leading to death.

Sir Thomas Malory wrote *Le Morte D'Arthur* whilst a political prisoner here in the fifteenth century. He was buried close by at Christ Church, Newgate Street (**see no.8**) after dying in the prison. Daniel Defoe began *Moll Flanders* here whilst a prisoner for debt, as was John Cleland, who wrote *Fanny Hill* at Newgate for twenty pounds to clear his debts. The twenty-three year old highwayman Jack Sheppard escaped from Newgate four times, the last after he was manacled to the floor of his cell in 'the Castle' several dangerous floors above ground.

The 'Condemned Hold' became a frequent place of entertainment when visitors paid to meet those sentenced to death. Guards would often write up the lives of those condemned, sometimes with the help of the inmate themselves. These became known as the 'Newgate Calendar'.

During the anti-Catholic Gordon Riots of 1780, Newgate was burnt and though many were left screaming inside, over three hundred prisoners were freed to roam the streets chained, bemused and lost.

When the riots had been subdued, the leader, Lord George Gordon, was himself imprisoned at Newgate where eventually he died from 'Gaol Fever' in 1793.

In 1783 the main public execution site moved to Newgate after crowds at Tyburn had become uncontrollable. The change of site however did not improve behaviour, as in 1802, during one execution, forty thousand spectators stampeded leaving over a hundred dead.

It was here, in 1820, that the five Cato Street Conspirators (**see p.12**), who had planned to assassinate the government, were the last to be beheaded after their death by hanging, the executioner using a surgeon's knife.

Dickens was a frequent visitor to Newgate and placed several scenes from his novels within its walls: particularly *Barnaby Rudge*, *Oliver Twist* when Fagin awaits death in the Condemned Hold and *Great Expectations* when Pip is shown the yard.

"They passed through several strong gates opened from the inner side; and having entered an open yard ascended a flight of narrow steps and came into a passage with a row of strong doors…. The condemned criminal was seated on his bed, rocking himself from side to side, with a countenance like that of a snared beast through the face of a man. His mind was evidently wondering to his old life for he continued muttering without appearing conscious of their presence otherwise than as a part of his vision."

DICKENS, *Oliver Twist*

In 1868 public hangings were abolished and all executions were moved inside the prison walls. The 'long drop' was introduced whereby a prisoner stood on a trap floor which, when it opened, caused him to fall eight feet, the rope breaking his neck immediately. Death was estimated to take a maximum of twenty seconds.

At its height, twenty people could be hanged on the Newgate gallows at one time. The last execution was that of George Woolf in 1902 for the gruesome murder of his girlfriend.

The prison was demolished in 1902. In its place was built the new Central Criminal Court (**see no.6**), utilising many of the old prison's stones.

"Those dreadful walls of Newgate which have hidden so much misery and such unspeakable anguish from the thoughts of men…." DICKENS, *Oliver Twist*

21│ Pudding Lane EC3

The Great Fire of London began in the kitchen of a bakery here on 2 September 1666. As most houses were built of wood and the weather was dry, the fire spread quickly. It lasted three days and destroyed much of the city.

22| Saffron Hill EC1

Until it was cleaned up in the mid-nineteenth century, Saffron Hill, along with Clerkenwell (**see no.10**), was a notorious criminal area. The nearby sewage-infested Fleet Ditch (now Farringdon Street) provided both a path and escape route for criminals between the two 'safe' areas.

"And so into Saffron Hill.... Although Oliver had enough to occupy his attention in keeping sight of his leader, he could not help bestowing a few hasty glances on either side, as he passed along. A dirty or more wretched place he had never seen. The street was very narrow and muddy and the air was impregnated with filthy odours.... The safe places that seemed to prosper amid the general blight of the place were the public houses and in them the lowest orders.... Covered ways and yards which here and there diverged from the main street, little knots of houses where drunken men and women were positively wallowing in filth." DICKENS, Oliver Twist

23| St Bartholomew's Hospital West Smithfield EC1

Founded in the twelfth century, this is London's oldest hospital. In 1381, Wat Tyler, leader of the Peasants' Revolt, fled here after being stabbed by

ST BARTHOLOMEW'S
HOSPITAL
THE OLD GATEWAY ENTRANCE

the Lord Mayor at Smithfield Market (**see no.28**). He was followed here by soldiers of the King and beheaded at the entrance to the hospital.

24| St Martin's le Grand EC1

Until 1697 the monastery that stood here provided the largest and safest sanctuary in England. Sanctuary was an ancient ecclesiastical right to protect those who came within the bounds of a church. It was a relic of the times when church law was as powerful as the laws of the state.

Prisoners on their way to execution at Tower Hill passed the gates of St Martin's. Sometimes, if they fought desperately enough, or if they had bribed their guards sufficiently, they were able to free themselves and enter the church. They were then safe as long as they remained there. Unless they were Jews or traitors, in which case the clergy turned them away.

One of the most famous to seek sanctuary here was Miles Forrest, who had been accused of the murder of the Princes in the Tower in 1483 (**see no.32**). Despite many attempts to evict him, Forrest stayed within the monastery until his death several years later.

25| St Mary's Church Aldermanbury EC2

Only the foundations remain of the church where Judge Jeffries was buried.

One of the most cruel of judges, Jeffries was the main instrument of fear used by the State during the reigns of Charles II and his brother James II. His judgements were particularly brutal during the anti-Protestant Popish Plot of 1678 and the savage punishments given out after Monmouth's Rebellion of 1685. He was Lord Chancellor when James II was overthrown and his unpopularity was such that he was arrested (**see p.82**) and left in the Tower of London to die.

26| St Paul's Churchyard EC4

This road passing by St Paul's Cathedral was once a place of execution. Many of the condemned were religious martyrs and included some of the conspirators of the Gunpowder Plot (**see p.61**) who were hanged, drawn and quartered outside no.37.

27| St Sepulchre Church Holborn Viaduct EC1

The bells of nearby St Sepulchre Church tolled when a prisoner was taken to Tyburn or executed at Newgate prison. Since 1605, a bequest had ensured that the night before an execution, a hand-bell would be brought by a priest through a tunnel linking the church to the condemned cell. Here twelve times the bell would be rung and the words chanted:

"Watch and pray the hour draws near
That you before the Almighty must appear
All you that in the Condemned Hold lie
Prepare you, for tomorrow you shall die."

The bell still survives and although the tunnel is bricked up, the entrance is still visible.

It was also from the church that nosegays were given to the prisoners on their way to execution.

28│ Smithfield Market Smithfield Street EC1

Smithfield was originally open land where cattle were brought to market. It was a dangerous place with the animals often stampeding through the nearby streets. It was also dirty with the blood and offal from the carcasses literally swamping the ground.

For over four hundred years it was used as a place of execution. The main London gallows stood here until 1400 when hangings moved to Tyburn. Smithfield then became a place for death by burning, a sentence given for witchcraft and heresy. These deaths took place outside the gateway of St Bartholomew the Great and were popular with spectators as the victims were burnt, boiled or roasted alive. In 1538, John Forest, a prior of a convent in Greenwich, drew particularly large crowds when he was placed in a cage and burnt alive for refusing to recognise the King's supremacy.

In total three hundred people were burnt during the sixteenth century, two hundred of these between 1554 and 1558 on the orders of Queen Mary I.

Two unfortunates were Bishops Ridley and Latimer, whom the fires burnt horribly but failed to kill as not enough wood had been used. The bishops spent several days in agony before death released them.

Excavations near the church in 1849 revealed the charred bones of the victims, many of which were then taken away as relics.

In 1381, the fourteen year old King Richard II met the leader of the Peasants' Revolt, Wat Tyler, at Smithfield.

It was a time of famine and Tyler's forces were rioting against the taxes raised to finance the wars with France. Travelling from Essex and Kent, the rebels entered London, opening up Marshalsea and Fleet Prisons, burning records at the Chancery and New Temple, amongst other properties. Many unpopular figures of authority were attacked and killed, including lawyers, the Lord Treasurer and the Archbishop of Canterbury. Richard II had taken refuge in the Tower of London.

Eventually however the King met Tyler at Smithfield where the rebels' demands so angered the mayor, William Walworth, that he stabbed Tyler in the neck with a knife. (The twelve-inch ridged dagger can be seen by appointment in the Fishmongers' Hall, Upper Thames Street EC4.) Tyler staggered to St Bartholomew's Hospital but was dragged out and finally killed by the King's forces. Walworth was knighted on the spot and given £100 by Richard. With Tyler dead, the rebellion soon ended.

29│ Sweeny Todd Barber's Shop 186 Fleet Street EC4
This was the place of work of the mythical barber who cut the throats of his customers. Their bodies were then turned into meat pies by his wife in nearby Bell Yard.

30│ Temple Bar Fleet Street EC4
The gateway marks the western boundary of the City of London. From 1684 to 1746 it was used to display the heads and other body parts of traitors.

Beside the gate stood a pillory in which Daniel Defoe (author of *Robinson Crusoe*) spent several days in 1703 for libel.

31│ Tower Hill EC3
A stone in the pavement by Trinity Square gardens marks the spot where at least seventy-five people were executed for treason. Though in fact many of them had been condemned for no more than falling from the ruling monarch's favour.

The first was Richard II's tutor, Simon de Burley, in 1388. Other significant executions included Henry VIII's most powerful ministers Sir Thomas More and Sir Thomas Cromwell, and the Protectors of Edward VI, the Dukes of Somerset and Northumberland.

In 1686, the illegitimate son of Charles II and the pretender to the throne, the Duke of Monmouth, was beheaded by Jack Ketch. Ketch, the six foot seven, eighteen stone incompetent, gave his name to all subsequent executioners after failing to behead Monmouth with three blows of the axe and resorting to the humiliation of a knife.

After the Duke's death, it was discovered that there was no portrait and being of royal blood, this needed immediate correction. So the hacked head was washed and crudely sewn back to the body when an artist worked through the night. The portrait can be seen at the National Portrait Gallery, with a ruff covering the sick-looking Duke's throat.

When Lord Lovat, one of the leaders of the 1745 Jacobite Rebellion, was executed in 1747, the spectator stand collapsed, killing twelve people. Lovat was the last person to be beheaded in England. (Beheading was formally abolished in 1814). So popular was his execution that the artist William Hogarth sold over ten thousand copies of his print of the execution, at a

shilling a time, within one week of Lovat's death.

The last execution at Tower Hill was in 1780, that of an one-armed soldier who had taken part in the Gordon Riots.

32 | **Tower of London** Tower Hill EC3
Tel. 0171-709 0765
Open daily 9am-6pm
Admission charge

This Norman castle has been used throughout the centuries as a royal palace, mint, zoo and prison. It was first used as a prison in 1101, because its position and secure buildings made it easy to keep captives. Ironically the first prisoner, the Bishop of Durham, imprisoned for selling benefices, escaped though his cell window after making his guards drunk.

- In 1278, six hundred Jews were held prisoner at the Tower for clipping coins, of whom, over two hundred were hanged the next year.
- The Traitors' Gate was built in 1285 to admit prisoners to the Tower via the safety of the Thames.
- In 1345 King John II of France was taken prisoner and held at the Tower for three years whilst France struggled to raise the ransom for his release.
- During the Peasants' Revolt of 1381, several of the King's ministers were held here before their execution at Tower Hill by the rebels.
- The Bloody Tower gained its name after the murder of the 'Princes in the Tower', the boy King Edward V and his brother, in 1483 (probably on the orders of their uncle, Richard III). They had been imprisoned in the tower after being declared illegitimate.
- During the early seventeenth century, Thomas Overbury was imprisoned and then poisoned here. Overbury was part of a homosexual triangle that consisted of himself, James I and Lord Rochester. Indeed it was a common joke at court that 'Rochester ruled the King and Overbury ruled Rochester'. Overbury's fall came when he became jealous and started to cause trouble when Rochester planned to marry the

Countess of Essex. Two years later, an apothecary confessed to the murder and implicated the Countess of Essex. She and her husband were charged. Their sentence of death was reprieved, but the couple were forced to live together at the Tower for seven years, at the end of which they hated each other.

● It was during the reign of Henry VIII that the Tower gained its reputation as a harsh prison. Those who refused to take the oath of supremacy (a capital offence) were sent here, as were two of the King's wives, Anne Boleyn and Catherine Howard, both executed for adultery. When Howard was brought to the Tower, she passed the head of her lover, Thomas Culpepper, already executed and displayed on London Bridge. Just before her own execution she said: "If I had married the man I loved instead of being dazzled by ambition, all would have been well. I die a Queen but I would rather have died the wife of Culpepper."

● In 1554, the pretender to the throne, Lady Jane Grey, was executed on the orders of Mary I. Another pretender, Mary Queen of Scots, was messily executed here in 1585, after three blows were required to sever her head.

● During the First World War, eleven spies were executed by firing squad near the Martin Tower. And Rudolf Hess spent four days imprisoned here during the Second World War, after he had flown into England in an attempt to negotiate a peace settlement.

Many of the victims' bodies are buried in the Tower precinct, in the Royal Chapel of St Peter ad Vincula, including Sir Thomas More, Bishop Fisher, Thomas Cromwell, Anne Boleyn and Catherine Howard.

33 | Unilever House (Bridewell Palace) Victoria Embankment EC4

This was once a royal palace where Henry VIII held negotiations to obtain a divorce from Catherine of Aragon. The failure of these talks led to the break with Rome and the formation of the Church of England.

In 1556 the palace became a prison for short-term inmates. Outside the walls, public floggings took place twice a week with the whipping continuing until the President of the Court banged his hammer on the table when he considered that the prisoners had had enough.

A ducking stool was installed in 1628 on the banks of the Thames. Here at high tide, the victims would be strapped into the chair and submerged beneath the water, often for minutes at a time. Stocks were introduced in 1638.

In 1788 straw beds were provided, so instantly making Bridewell one of the most forward looking prisons in the country. As no other prison provided either bed or bedding, this was not difficult.

When the prison was demolished in 1855, the inmates were transferred to Holloway.

34 | The Viaduct Tavern 126 Newgate Street EC1

The cellars of this Victorian pub, opposite the Old Bailey, were once dungeons of the old Newgate prison.

PUNISHMENTS

PUNISHMENT IS THE OLDEST FORM OF ENFORCING THE LAW. BEFORE THE USE OF PRISONS, IT WAS THE ONLY ALTERNATIVE TO FINES AND EXECUTION. THE MOST POPULAR FORM OF PUNISHMENT WAS FLOGGING AND IT WAS THE LONGEST-LASTING, STILL USED IN PRISONS IN ENGLAND UNTIL 1948. MOST FORMS OF PUNISHMENT HAD CEASED BY THE END OF THE EIGHTEENTH CENTURY.

AMONGST THE MANY FORMS OF PUNISHMENT USED WERE:

STOCKS AND PILLORIES

STOCKS (SITTING) AND PILLORIES (STANDING) WERE MOSTLY USED FOR MINOR CRIMES SUCH AS DRUNKENNESS, BLASPHEMY AND CHEATING. THE OFFENDER COULD REMAIN CONFINED FOR SEVERAL DAYS AND COULD DIE FROM THE ABUSE SUFFERED. THE STOCKS WERE LAST USED IN 1872.

BRANDING

BRANDING WAS CARRIED OUT WITH A HOT IRON AND WAS OFTEN A PUNISHMENT ACCOMPANYING MUTILATION. THE VICTIM WOULD BE MARKED WITH A SIGN OR LETTER DISTINGUISHING HIS CRIME. THUS A THIEF COULD BEAR A 'T' ON HIS FOREHEAD OR CHEEK, AS WELL AS HAVING HIS NOSE REMOVED. THE LAST BRANDING TOOK PLACE IN 1799.

WHIPPING AND FLOGGING

WHIPPING WAS THE MOST FREQUENT FORM OF PUNISHMENT, WITH THE CAT O'NINE TAILS OR BULL WHIP USED TO FLAY THE SKIN AS THE VICTIM WAS LED THROUGH THE STREETS.

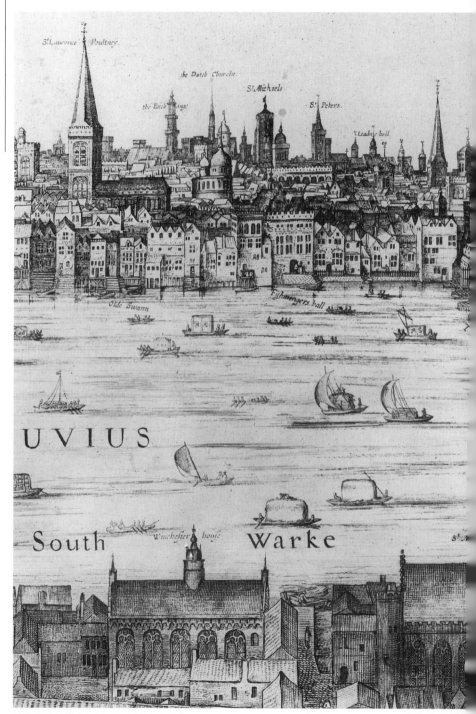

LONDON BRIDGE WITH THE HEADS OF TRAITORS ON DISPLAY

St. Dunston in the east

St. Hellen

St. Andrew

Billingat

Bridge Gate

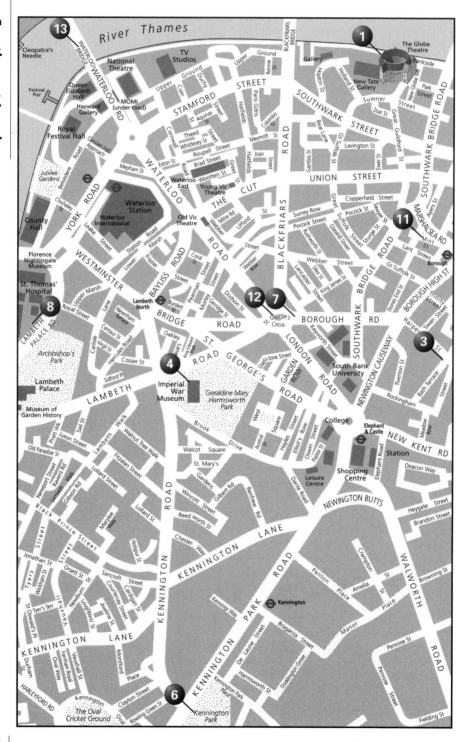

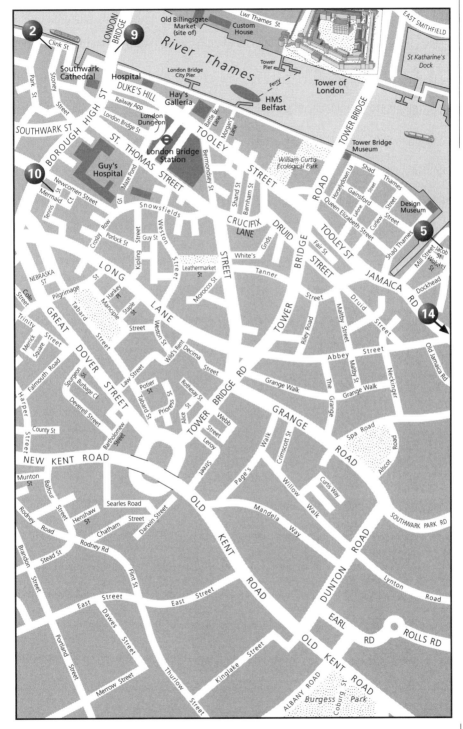

South-east London

Lambeth, Waterloo, Southwark and Deptford

PROSTITUTION

KNOWN AS THE 'OLDEST PROFESSION', PROSTITUTION WAS COMMONPLACE DURING THE ROMAN SETTLEMENT IN LONDON. AND IN THE EARLY CHRISTIAN PERIOD, IT WAS MARGINALISED UNDER THE PREVALENT AUSTERE ATTITUDE OF ST AUGUSTINE WHO BELIEVED, 'JUST AS SEWERS WERE NEEDED TO CARRY AWAY LIQUIDS AND WASTE SO PROSTITUTES WERE ALSO NECESSARY'.

PROSTITUTION WAS HEAVILY TAXED AND IT GREW UP ONLY IN CONTROLLED AREAS, MOST COMMONLY WHERE SHIPS DOCKED OR AT ENTRANCES TO LONDON AND PLACES OF ENTERTAINMENT. IN 1506, THERE WERE EIGHTEEN LICENSED BROTHELS AT BANKSIDE AND COCK LANE IN SMITHFIELD.

DURING THE FIFTEENTH CENTURY BECAUSE OF THE GROWING PREVALENCE OF SYPHILIS, CHILD BROTHELS EMERGED. THE PERCEIVED CLEANLINESS OF THE SEVEN TO FOURTEEN YEAR OLD INMATES COMMANDED A MUCH HIGHER PRICE.

THE MASSIVE URBANISATION AND INDUSTRIAL GROWTH OF LONDON OF THE EIGHTEENTH AND NINETEENTH CENTURIES SAW AN EQUALLY LARGE RISE IN THE NUMBERS OF BROTHELS AND PROSTITUTES TO SERVICE THE RISING POPULATION. BY 1857 THERE WERE SIX THOUSAND BROTHELS AND EIGHTY THOUSAND PROSTITUTES IN LONDON.

London has always been a city based on trade and merchants always need entertainment. Here Bankside, on the approach to, but beyond the authority of, the City, came into its own.

Owned and controlled by the church, the area provided brothels, bull and bear baiting, theatres, gaming and taverns. All above board, licensed and taxed. But go too far and the Clink was only around the corner, providing various levels of imprisonment and punishment, from flogging to the pillory, to torture and the bottomless pit.

It was rightly said that along the south bank, all of life's variety could be seen and as much of death that you could stomach.

1 | Bankside SE1

Since London was first inhabited by the Romans over two thousand years ago, Bankside has been a place of entertainment and often infamy.

The Romans were the first to build bath-houses beside the southern approach to London's oldest bridge. Here, outside the control of the civic authorities, merchants and visitors would stay. As is the way, prostitution soon developed and continued over the next centuries.

In medieval times, animal sports became popular, including bear and bull baiting. During the Elizabethan period, the theatres were added and the area became known as Stew's (Prostitute's) Bank, the prostitutes often being recently arrived immigrants.

The area was tightly controlled by the Bishops of Winchester. Nobody could operate without a licence and infringements to the rules were punished with fines and incarceration at the Clink (**see no.2**). The prostitutes lived under a strict set of regulations and, if venereal diseases were suspected, were immediately cast out.

On the corner of Southwark and Redcross Streets there was an unconsecrated graveyard for the area's prostitutes.

2 | Clink Prison Museum 1 Clink Street SE1
Tel. 0171-378 1558
Open daily 10am-6pm
Admission charge

The museum is on the site of a small sixteenth century prison called the Clink. The prison was part of the palace of the Bishops of Winchester. The original site was a little to the east and was used to punish errant clerics. However as the area developed into a place of entertainment, the Clink more frequently housed actors, pimps, prostitutes and their unruly customers.

There was a separate women's prison, until 1465, standing on today's Cathedral Street, at the Great Gate to the Bishop's Palace. Here the inmates, mostly prostitutes, could be further punished by being placed in a pillory or being submerged in the Thames tied to a ducking stool which, because of the filthy state of the river, could prove fatal.

CLINK PRISON MUSEUM
DEDICATED TO THE HORRORS OF
PRISON LIFE AND TORTURE

Below the Great Hall of the palace was a further place of confinement known as the 'Fure'. It was dark, damp and forgotten. Here those without hope of release were imprisoned and left to rot.

The prison was little used after the Civil War, except for debtors. It was burnt down during the anti-Catholic Gordon Riots of 1780.

The present museum has displays of prison life and torture.

3 | Horsemonger Lane Gaol Sessions House Gardens, Harper Road SE1
This was the site of an eighteenth century prison where public executions took place.

In 1849 a Mr and Mrs Manning were executed for the murder of a friend whom they had buried under their kitchen floor. Charles Dickens attended the hanging in November and was so outraged by the crowds, that he wrote to The Times the following day: "I don't believe any community can prosper where such a scene of horror as was enacted outside Horsemonger Lane Gaol is permitted. The horrors of the gibbet and of the crime which brought the wretched murderers to it faded in my mind before the atrocious bearing, looks and language of the assembled spectators." His letter created a ground-swell of opinion that eventually led to the end of public executions.

4 | Imperial War Museum Lambeth Road SE1
Tel. 0171-416 5000
Open daily 10am-6pm
Admission charge
The main body of this building is all that is left of the former Bethlehem Royal Hospital. The hospital was more commonly known as Bedlam. It was

IMPERIAL WAR MUSEUM

ORIGINALLY BEDLAM HOSPITAL
FOR THE CRIMINALLY INSANE

established in 1247 in the City of London (**see p.35**) to house 'distracted' patients and moved here in 1815, where a separate division was created to house the criminally insane. However, in 1864, they were moved outside London, to Broadmoor Prison.

Until very recently, mental illness was much misunderstood with patients given little sympathy. If they were passive, they were left in isolation and if not, they could be chained to walls almost permanently. The prevalent attitude was that they were freaks and it became a fashionable pastime to view the inmates in their caged confinement for the payment of a small fee.

Amongst the many who stayed at Bedlam over the years were:

● Edward Oxford, who spent twenty-four years here for his attempt to assassinate Queen Victoria, spending his time industriously, learning five languages before his release and emigration to Australia;

● Daniel McNaughton, who in 1843 tried to assassinate the Prime Minister, Robert Peel, but missed, killing his secretary Edward Drummond instead; and

● Richard Dadd, considered the greatest painter of his generation until, in 1843, he killed his father near the Serpentine Lake in Hyde Park believing him to be the devil. His famous fairy paintings (displayed in the Tate Gallery) were painted here, during his forty years of incarceration.

In 1930 the hospital moved, again, to its present site, Beckenham, Kent.

5| Jacob Street SE1

Here amid today's desirable apartments are the warehouses that made up one of the worst slums of the nineteenth century. The residents nearly all suffered from cholera, caught from the adjacent Neckinger River, with crime and begging providing the main source of income.

Dickens used the area in *Oliver Twist* as the site where the thug Bill Sykes dies after fleeing the murder of his girlfriend Nancy.

6| Kennington Park Kennington Park Road SE11

St Mark's Church was the site of the eighteenth century gallows for the county of Surrey. Indeed during repair work to the church, the base of a gibbet was found beneath the crypt.

In 1745, many Jacobite rebels were hanged here before being beheaded and displayed at Temple Bar **(see p.41)**. The fiancee of one of the rebels, James Dawson, was so overcome with grief that she died of a stroke whilst watching him hang.

7| King's Bench Prison St George's Circus SE1

Borough High Street was the site of this prison from the sixteenth century, used mainly to house debtors, including in 1752 the King of Corsica. As with most of the prisons in London, the condition of the inmates depended very much on their ability to raise private finance. The warders would give them great leeway with regard to food, visits and accommodation. Even women and a luxurious life could be maintained if one had sufficient funds. However, those without money were frequently left heavily chained and starved.

In 1754 an enquiry revealed corruption and the prison moved to St George's Fields **(see no.12)**. But the old habits continued and it soon became known as the most desirable place of incarceration in London with wealthy prisoners able to buy the freedom to move within a three mile radius of the prison.

When imprisonment for debt was abolished, the prison was turned over to the military and demolished in 1880.

8| 103 Lambeth Palace Road SE1

Home of Thomas Cream, whose murders, before he was discovered, were thought to have been the work of Jack the Ripper. Cream was a doctor who poisoned at least four prostitutes: in October 1891, Matilda Clover at her brothel at 27 Lambeth Road; Ellen Donworth, in Waterloo Road, a few days earlier; and in April 1892, Emma Shrivell and Alice Marsh, at 118 Stamford Street.

Cream's downfall came when he attempted to blackmail a fellow doctor, Joseph Harper, whose son also lived at 103 Lambeth Palace Road and, Cream claimed, had committed the murders. The police were informed. Cream was investigated when it was discovered he had served ten years in prison in America for poisoning, and charged. He was hanged at Newgate on 15 November 1892.

9│ London Bridge SE1

London Bridge marks the first crossing of the Thames in London.

In 1305 the gruesome tradition began of placing heads and body parts of traitors on display at the south gate, Traitors' Gate. After execution, heads were taken to the gatehouse where they were boiled and then dipped in tar for preservation. This was intended to deter all those who might enter London from committing a crime.

The first was that of Scottish rebel, William Wallace (the character played by Mel Gibson in the film *Braveheart*).

Amongst the many heads displayed were those of rebel leader Jack Cade in 1450, Bishop John Fisher and Sir Thomas More in 1535, Thomas Cromwell in 1540 and Guy Fawkes and the conspirators of the gunpowder plot in 1606. The last head was displayed in 1678.

10│ Marshalsea Prison Marshalsea Gardens, off Angel Place SE1

The Marshalsea Prison was named after the court presided over by the King's Marshal. The original prison stood by Mermaid Court but was destroyed in the 1381 Peasants' Revolt.

During Elizabeth I's reign, the rebuilt prison became second in importance only to the Tower and in the late eighteenth century it moved to just north of St George's Church. Here stood the prison that Charles Dickens knew so well, his father having been incarcerated at Marshalsea for debt. The effect of visiting his father so affected Dickens that prison loomed strongly throughout his novels, with the eponymous heroine of *Little Dorrit* born in the Marshalsea.

The prison closed in 1842 and the present Marshalsea Gardens were constructed on part of the prison courtyard.

11│ Mint Street SE1

This area until the early nineteenth century was a labyrinth of dirty, narrow alleys. During the eighteenth century, the area was particularly notorious as a base for criminals. At one time or another, all the rogues of the age would visit. The highwayman Jack Sheppard hid here before his arrest and after his frequent escapes from prison. As did Jonathan Wild, the undisputed leader of the London underworld between 1712 and 1725.

Wild lived in a large house on the site of 30 Old Bailey EC4. Outwardly he was a 'thief-taker', a sort-of prototype detective who was paid up to £2500 for turning in thieves and rogues. Indeed he advertised himself as 'the Thief-taker General of all England'.

But Wild was playing the system every way. Starting out as a pimp, he was England's first major mobster, pioneering organised crime. Wild controlled a vast group of criminals: specially trained thieves to rob at court, highwaymen, burglars, pickpockets and prostitutes. And at his height, most of London's seven thousand criminals either worked for him indirectly or lived in fear of the consequences. At least a hundred of those who gave him trouble, he sent to the authorities for execution, with Wild, each time, riding at the head of their cart to Tyburn, shouting: 'make way for my children!' Even in his condemned cell at Newgate when he was eventually caught, he continued to operate his empire.

As he arrived at his own hanging, the crowds mocked him with cries of 'make way for our father!'. But Wild was beyond comprehension, drugged as he was on opium. It was not until his body was stripped naked that the crowds could see the nineteen sword and pistol scars over his body; Wild had been frequently attacked during his lifetime. What was not seen were the several silver plates that held his skull together in places where many fractures over the years had weakened it.

After his execution, Wild's skeleton was taken to the Royal College of Surgeons, where it remains, and his warehouses filled with stolen goods reverted to the Treasury.

12 | St George's Circus SE1

In the eighteenth century, the land surrounding this area was open fields, known as St George's Fields.

Here on 2 June 1780, fifty thousand people gathered to begin a march on Parliament under the leadership of Lord George Gordon. They wished to protest against the repeal of anti-Catholic legislation. However as they travelled through London, the march ran out of control.

Property was looted and most London prisons were broken into and the prisoners freed before the buildings were set alight. In the ensuing mayhem the army attempted to restore order, resulting in the death of eight hundred and fifty people. Gordon was later arrested and sent to Newgate.

Charles Dickens described the riots in *Barnaby Rudge*.

"... for in half an hour or less, the rioters, having previously prevented the lighting of the street lamps, rose like a great sea; ... one after another, new fires blazed up in every quarter of the town, as though it were the intention of the insurgents to wrap the city in a circle of flames. ... The crowd swarmed and roared in every street. ... In two hours, six-and-thirty fires were raging: among them the Borough Clink in Tooley Street, the King's Bench, the Fleet, and the New Bridewell. In almost every street there was a battle; and in every quarter the muskets of the troops were heard above the shouts and tumult of the mob. The firing began in the Poultry, where the chain was drawn across the road, where nearly a score of people were killed on the first discharge. ... The streets were now a dreadful spectacle. The shouts of the rabble, the shrieks of women, the cries of the wounded, and the constant firing, formed a deafening and an awful accompaniment to the sights which every corner presented. ... There was hot work and bloodshed in almost every leading thoroughfare."

13| Waterloo Bridge SE1

One of the most mysterious deaths that led to great diplomatic embarrassment was the murder of Georgi Markov in 1978.

Markov fled Bulgaria in 1969 and worked as a broadcaster for the BBC and Radio Free Europe. His work so inflamed the Bulgarian authorities that an agent was dispatched to terminate the problem.

As Markov walked to work across Waterloo Bridge, on 7 September 1978, he felt a prick in his leg. A man with an umbrella mumbled an apology and hurried away. Later that evening Markov collapsed. The doctors could find no cause and he died the following day. However an autopsy revealed that a poison had been administered via his leg. The umbrella had disguised a hypodermic needle. Despite clear links to the Bulgarian Secret Police, all the investigations came to nothing against the wall of diplomatic immunity.

14| Deptford Strand SE8

off map: nearest station Surrey Quays

Here, the playwright and poet, Christopher Marlowe, was murdered. At the age of twenty-nine, he was the author of *Tamberlaine the Great*, *Dr Faustus* and *The Passionate Shepherd* and was Shakespeare's greatest rival. But he had also been involved in political espionage.

On 30 May 1593, he visited a tavern on the waterfront here with three friends, one of whom was Ingram Frezer, the servant of Sir Thomas Walsingham, head of Queen Elizabeth I's secret service. They had been drinking all day. Frezer alleged that after disputing the bill, Marlowe attacked him and in defence he stabbed the playwright above the eye, killing him instantly.

However it is thought that Marlowe was killed on the orders of the government to keep his views on atheism silent. As he had been an anti-Catholic spy, putting him on trial for his atheism might have led to the disclosure of embarrassing secrets.

Within hours, Marlowe was buried in an unmarked grave in the churchyard of St Nicholas at Deptford Green, just behind Creek Road. And Frezer was charged with only a breech of the peace.

The human skull and bones sitting on the wall of St Nicholas's, known to locals as the sailor's church, were adopted by pirates as the symbol on their flag, the Skull and Cross Bones.

St Nicholas's Church BURIAL PLACE OF THE MURDERED PLAYWRIGHT MARLOWE

BANQUETING HOUSE THE EXECUTION OF KING CHARLES I IN 1649

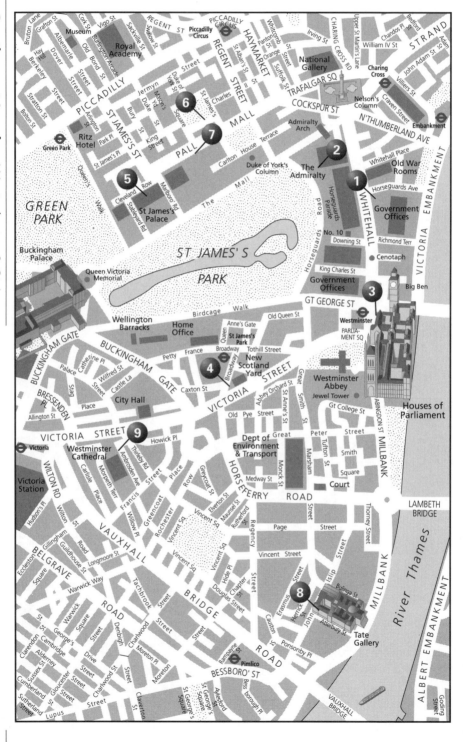

South-west London
Westminster & St James

Today the borough of Westminster boasts the seat of government, two cathedrals and three royal palaces. Tourists flock to watch the changing of the guard outside Buckingham Palace and to watch Big Ben chime the hour.

But in the past the area was a centre for punishment and execution of the most brutal kind. A cathedral and an art gallery now stand where notorious prisons once dominated the vista. And the Houses of Parliament have witnessed displays of tortuous punishments which they eventually banned by law for their brutality.

Members of royalty and government did not escape the grasp of horror. For it was here that a king was tried and executed and that a government minister was killed by terrorists.

1 | Banqueting House Whitehall SW1
Tel. 0171-930 4179
Open Mon-Sat 10am-5pm
Admission charge

On the freezing morning of 30 January 1649, Charles I made his last walk from St James's Palace, across the park, to the Banqueting House of Whitehall Palace. And there, from under the gloriously painted ceiling, he stepped onto a balcony constructed on the street for his execution.

The huge crowds were silent as he professed his innocence of all charges laid against him by Parliament. He then knelt and instructed the executioner to proceed. He wore two thick undershirts to prevent shivering in front of the crowd. For Charles, as King, did not tremble at anything, even death.

The King's head was displayed to the crowd before later being sewn back to the body for burial at Windsor Castle.

2 | Citadel The Mall SW1
This bomb-proof bunker was built to withstand the heaviest bombing of the Second World War. It stands beside the Admiralty to provide shelter and communication rooms, thirty feet below ground. And today is part of a system that still provides defence should London be attacked.

3 | Houses of Parliament Parliament Square SW1
Tel. 0171-219 4272
Open: access to the public gallery during parliamentary debates
Free

As the seat of government from Saxon times, the Houses of Parliament have seen their fair share of horror over the centuries.

Perhaps the most significant event was the trial and sentencing of Charles I in Westminster Hall in 1649, when the King was condemned to death after failing in his attempt to assert his demand for absolute power over Parliament. (**See no.1 for his execution**).

THE BLITZ

BETWEEN SEPTEMBER 1940 AND MAY 1941, THE NAZIS TRIED TO BOMB LONDON INTO SUBMISSION THROUGH A 'BLITZKRIEG' (A LIGHTNING WAR).

USING THE THAMES AS A NAVIGATIONAL PATH, A TOTAL OF NINETEEN THOUSAND TONNES OF HIGH EXPLOSIVES WERE DROPPED. LONDONERS HID IN HASTILY ERECTED SHELTERS, BASEMENTS AND UNDERGROUND STATIONS. BUT STILL FIFTEEN THOUSAND PEOPLE WERE KILLED.

THREE AND A HALF MILLION BUILDINGS WERE DAMAGED OR DESTROYED, MAKING IT THE MOST DESTRUCTIVE EVENT IN THE HISTORY OF LONDON SINCE THE GREAT FIRE OF 1666.

THE EXECUTIONER OF KING
CHARLES I
WHO WAS BEHEADED OUTSIDE
THE BANQUETING HOUSE IN
JANUARY 1649

After the Restoration of the monarchy, the bodies of the Parliamentary leaders, including Oliver Cromwell, were dug up in 1661 in retaliation and gibbeted at Tyburn. Their rotting heads were then placed on spikes over the entrance to Westminster Hall and displayed for nearly twenty years.

On 11 May 1812, the Prime Minister, Spencer Percival, was entering the House of Commons, when he was surprised to see John Bellingham approach him. For many months the Liverpool merchant, living at 9 Millman Street WC1, had been haranguing him. Bellingham had been wrongfully arrested and held in Russia whilst on a business trip and wanted the government to support his claim for compensation against the Russians. But the Prime Minister wanted nothing to do with the man or the case.

Percival ignored Bellingham, but as he brushed past, Bellingham drew a gun and shot the Prime Minister dead. Consternation ensued. As Bellingham was whisked away an unprecedented security clamp down occurred in case it was part of a plot to unseat the government. The troops were called out to seal off London and all mail was stopped to paralyse communication. Only later was it discovered that the assassination was the work of one obsessed individual. Bellingham was hanged the following week at Newgate where Lord Byron wrote in his diary: "on sitting up all night, I saw Bellingham launched into eternity." His body was dissected at St Bartholomew's Hospital on the orders of the Court.

Just before the 1979 election that swept Margaret Thatcher's Conservative Government to power, the IRA carried out a series of atrocities to keep their profile high during the election campaign.

The most prominent and terrible of these was the assassination of one of

Thatcher's main political lieutenants and spokesman for Northern Ireland, Airey Neave. On the evening of 30 March 1979, Neave drove his car out of the underground car park. Midway up the ramp, the car exploded killing him immediately. The IRA claimed responsibility.

At the corner of Bridge Street and Parliament Square is New Palace Yard, the place of punishment for many centuries. Stocks and a pillory stood here until 1765.

The open space by the public entrance to the Houses of Parliament is Old Palace Yard, the site of Edward the Confessor's original palace and today used as a car park.

In 1606 Guy Fawkes and his fellow conspirators were executed in the yard for their part in the Gun Powder Plot. They had been caught on 5 November the previous year in the cellars beneath Parliament. The group of Catholics had intended to blow up the Government and King James I, and so put an end to Protestant rule.

Unfortunately, one of the group, Frances Tresham, warned his brother-in-law, a member of Parliament, not to attend that day. Suspicion arose and Guy Fawkes was discovered in the basement surrounded by barrels of gunpowder.

After being tortured at the Tower of London, the surviving conspirators were dragged through the streets and executed here. Their heads were then displayed on London Bridge as a warning.

In 1618, Sir Walter Raleigh was also executed here. Raleigh, a successful adventurer and explorer thirty years before, had fallen out of favour in 1603 when he was sentenced to death for plotting to place Arabella Stuart on the throne after Elizabeth I's death. The sentence was reprieved to imprisonment in the Tower of London. However he was released in 1617, after fourteen years, to captain an expedition to find gold in South America. When he returned empty handed, the original sentence was invoked and the old and broken Sir Walter Raleigh was executed.

TORTURE

TORTURE ONLY BECAME COMMONLY USED IN THE THIRTEENTH CENTURY. AFTER WITNESSING ITS SUCCESS DURING THE CRUSADES INTO THE HOLY LAND, THE COUNTRY'S RULERS BEGAN TO APPRECIATE ITS BENEFITS. IT WAS NOT SEEN AS A PUNISHMENT SO MUCH AS AN EFFICIENT WAY TO OBTAIN CONFESSIONS AND INFORMATION FROM RELUCTANT PRISONERS.

COMMON FORMS OF TORTURE WERE THE RACK, FOOT AND HAND CLAMPS, THE BURNING OF FLESH AND WEIGHTS PLACED ON THE BODY. TORTURE WAS WIDELY USED UNTIL THE MID-SEVENTEENTH CENTURY WHEN IT CEASED AS THE EVIDENCE IT PRODUCED BEGAN TO BE VIEWED AS UNRELIABLE.

THE HOUSES OF PARLIAMENT A SITE OF EXECUTION AND PUNISHMENT THROUGHOUT THE CENTURIES

HISTORY OF POLICING

UNTIL THE 1829 ACT OF PARLIAMENT WHICH ESTABLISHED THE BRITISH POLICE, A STATUTE DATING FROM 1285 HAD BEEN IN FORCE. THIS STATED THAT EVERY MAN BETWEEN THE AGES OF FIFTEEN AND SIXTY WAS ENTITLED TO MAINTAIN THE PEACE.

UNTIL THE FOURTEENTH CENTURY, LONDON HAD A CURFEW AND MEN PATROLLED THE GATES TO THE CITY, A SYSTEM BASED ON ROMAN PROCEDURE. HOWEVER, FROM THE SIXTEENTH CENTURY, WHEN ATTACK OF LONDON WAS LESS LIKELY, EACH WARD WAS GIVEN AUTHORITY TO PATROL ITS OWN DISTRICT FOR THE PURPOSES OF MAINTAINING LAW AND ORDER AT NIGHT. SO POLICING IN ENGLAND WAS ESSENTIALLY A SYSTEM OF NIGHTWATCHMEN OF VARYING EFFECTIVENESS, AGE AND ABILITY.

4| New Scotland Yard Broadway SW1

These are the headquarters of the Metropolitan Police Force. They were established at Old Scotland Yard (4 Whitehall Place, now demolished) in 1829 by Sir Robert Peel (hence the nicknames Bobbies and Peelers). The Yard contains a museum (open by appointment only) of crime and artefacts connected to some of England's most notorious criminals.

5| St James's Palace SW1

This was the site of a leper hospital until Henry VIII acquired it to build a palace.

Banned from the City of London, lepers were feared because of their ulceration and deformity. They were forced to carry bells and clappers to warn of their approach. The first recorded case of leprosy in England was that of the Bishop of London in 1087. Other illnesses, particularly syphilis, were often misdiagnosed as leprosy and, by the time Henry VIII bought the hospital, most inmates were suffering from syphilis.

6| 5 St James's Square SW1

From the window of the Libyan People's Bureau, Yvonne Fletcher, a twenty-five year old policewomen, was shot dead on 17 April 1984. She died only metres from her policeman fiance. Both were marshalling an anti-Gaddafi demonstration. The gunman was never charged as those in the building had diplomatic immunity.

7| Schomberg House 80-82 Pall Mall SW1

Before the development of modern medicine, the search for health lay

NEW SCOTLAND YARD
THE SIGN THAT SENDS TERROR THROUGH THE BONES OF TODAY'S CRIMINALS

SCHOMBERG HOUSE A PLACE OF MEDICAL EXPERIMENT IN THE EIGHTEENTH CENTURY

OVER THE YEARS AMATEUR GROUPS OF WATCHMEN AND PATROLS WERE ESTABLISHED. THE CITY OF LONDON BROUGHT IN A SORT OF NATIONAL SERVICE FOR EACH FREEMAN TO SERVE A YEAR AS A CONSTABLE OR BEADLE.

IN 1705 THE WATCH ACT CREATED A PAID, PROFESSIONAL WATCH FORCE.

THE CITY OF LONDON, BANKRUPTED BY THE GREAT FIRE OF 1666, DECIDED TO AUCTION THE POSTS OF MARSHALS. CORRUPTION ENSUED AS THE OFFICES CHANGED HANDS FREQUENTLY. THIS WAS WHEN THE 'THIEF-TAKERS' EMERGED, QUASI-BOUNTY HUNTERS. JONATHAN WILD WAS THE MOST WELL-KNOWN. IN 1778, THE CITY COULD AFFORD TO STOP THE SELLING OF OFFICES AND THEY REASSUMED CONTROL OF THE POSTS.

IN 1784, SHORTLY AFTER THE GORDON RIOTS, THE CITY CREATED A DAY PATROL, WHO CHOSE TO WEAR BLUE UNIFORMS AS THIS WAS A SOBER COLOUR IN WHICH TO ATTEND EXECUTIONS.

WHEN THE 1829 ACT ESTABLISHING A PROFESSIONAL POLICE FORCE CAME INTO BEING, THE POLICEMEN HAD TO WEAR THEIR UNIFORM ALL THE TIME, ON OR OFF DUTY. IT TOO WAS BLUE, TO DISTINGUISH THEM FROM THE MILITARY. THE CITY SET UP ITS OWN POLICE FORCE, WHICH IT MAINTAINS CONTROL OVER TO THIS DAY.

PUBLIC REACTION TO THE ESTABLISHMENT OF THE POLICE FORCE WAS HOSTILE FOR SEVERAL YEARS.

mostly in the hands of quacks. The medical establishment, without a proper understanding of hygiene and drugs, based their cures as much on superstition as on common sense. Surgery was conducted with as much finesse as butchery and the treatment for most ailments was bleeding.

Quacks proliferated. In the late eighteenth century, one of the most successful was a Scottish doctor, James Graham. Here, in this grand house, he established a fashionable clinic, called the 'Temple of Health and Hymen'. Society flocked to his expensive cures that included the early use of electric shock treatment. But more particularly to his famed 'celestial bed'. This was a huge structure, made ornately from gold and surrounded by mirrors with a mechanical music-box. The bed 'guaranteed' fertility and couples queued up to hire it and to see its use demonstrated by the naked and beautiful Emma Hart, who later became Lady Hamilton and the mistress of Admiral Nelson.

But quackery could be a precarious business and so it was for Graham, who ended his days destitute and confined to a lunatic asylum.

8 | Tate Gallery of Art Millbank SW1
Tel. 0171-887 8000
Open daily 10am-5.50pm
Free

Until 1890 this was the site of Millbank Penitentiary. It was built in 1821 as the largest prison in London. At its height it covered eighteen acres and contained eleven hundred cells. Although intended as a model prison, the bad air from the river and the marshy land upon which it was surrounded always made Millbank a place of ill health. Indeed, the writer Henry James, in the late nineteenth century, observed that the prison was "a worse act of violence than any it was erected to punish."

Many prisoners were housed at Millbank before being transported to Australia. And there is a prison bollard marking the spot where steps led to barges which took the prisoners to Wapping, the first stage of their journey. The tunnel through which they passed beneath the road began at the prison wall on the present site of the Morpeth Arms pub.

9 | Westminster Cathedral Victoria Street SW1
Tel. 0171-798 9055
Open daily 7am-8pm
Free

The late-nineteenth century Catholic cathedral was built on the site of Tothill Fields Prison. The fields stretched down to the river, covering much of today's Westminster and were popular with Londoners who flocked here to watch the bull and bear baiting, which took place in the area until 1820 and 1793 respectively. It was also a place of punishment, particularly for those accused of witchcraft. The area had also been used by Druids for the worship of the god, Teut, from which it partly derives its name.

During the Great Plague of 1664-65, local victims were buried in the fields, as were a thousand Scottish prisoners from the Battle of Worcester during the Civil War.

WESTMINSTER CATHEDRAL ONCE TOTHILL FIELDS PRISON

RUTH ELLIS THE LAST WOMAN TO BE HANGED IN BRITAIN

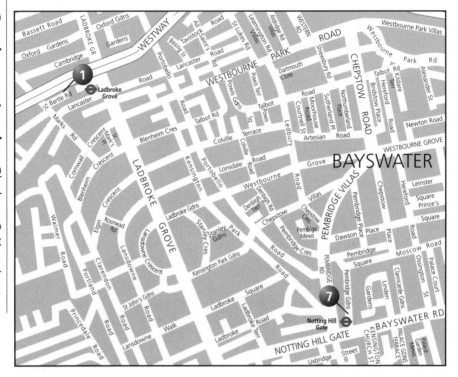

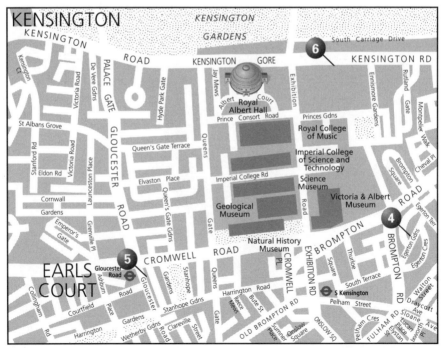

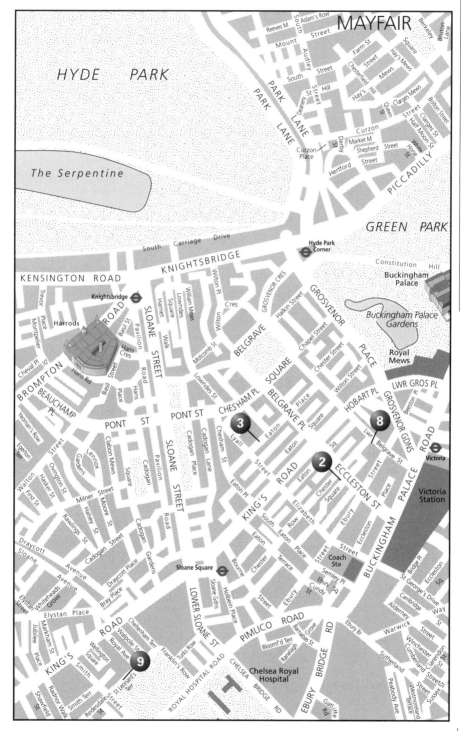

Chelsea & Kensington

Poverty, greed and desperation all drive people to crime.

Until very recently the population of London lived their life in close physical proximity to each other, even in the leafy and wealthy borough of Kensington and Chelsea. The elegant rows of houses and the smart streets belied a gentile calm.

From the richest to the poorest there was little room for the individual to move in public or in private.

Only in the late twentieth century came the developments that allowed greater individual living space and with it, some privacy. Unfortunately this could also lead to alienation and desperation. In extreme cases, along with the availability of poisons and chemicals, the terrible incidents of psychopathic murder, like those committed by John Christie and John Haigh.

1| **Bartle Road** (10 Rillington Place) W11

Here some of the most horrific and famed murders of the twentieth century took place. John Christie lived at 10 Rillington Place between 1938 and 1953. During this time, Christie, a Special Constable during the Second World War, murdered seven or eight women after brutally sexually assaulting them. He buried their bodies about the property, including, in 1952, his wife beneath the floorboards.

In 1948 the wife of Timothy Evans, another lodger in the property, and their infant daughter were found dead in Christie's garden shed. Evans was mentally subnormal and confessed to the crime before being hanged at Pentonville.

It was not until another body was found by a Jamaican tenant in 1953 that Christie was charged and Timothy Evans was discovered to have been innocent. Christie hanged at Pentonville later that year.

JOHN CHRISTIE

THE SERIAL MURDERER ON HIS

WAY TO JAIL

CHESTER SQUARE (LEFT) AND
ST LEONARD'S TERRACE
(RIGHT)
HOMES OF LONDON'S FAMOUS
HORROR WRITERS

2| 24 Chester Square SW1

This was the last home of Mary Shelley, who died here in 1851. Her most famous book, *Frankenstein,* was a huge success when published in 1818. The horror story of the man-made monster created from dead bodies has inspired many films and is recognised as the prototype science-fiction novel. It is thought that much of the work was based upon the macabre images stemming from her years using drugs with the poets Lord Byron and her husband Percy Bysshe Shelley. However many of the images also reflect her familiarity with death from her mother's attempted suicide on Putney Bridge and the death of many of her own children in infancy.

After her death at Chester Square, Mary was buried in Bournemouth along with the preserved heart of her husband, who had died thirty years previously. Shelley had drowned in Italy in 1822 and his heart had been snatched from the funeral pyre by the author Edward Trelawny, an act which severely burnt his hand.

3| 36 Eaton Place SW1

On 22 June 1922, Sir Henry Wilson died on the pavement outside his home in Eaton Place. He was the senior government advisor for the fight against terrorism in Northern Ireland. Despite heavy security, the two IRA men were able to shoot the MP and escape. However the terrorists, Reginald Dunn and Joseph O'Sullivan, were caught when passers by chased them down Ebury Street.

4| 44 Egerton Gardens SW3

At Holloway prison, on 13 July 1955, Ruth Ellis was the last woman to be executed in England.

Ellis was a twenty-nine year old single mother, who managed a private drinking club at 37 Brompton Road. She became the lover of a twenty-five year old playboy, David Blakely, who moved into her bedsit at Egerton Gardens.

During the few stormy months of their relationship, Ellis had at least two abortions and became unstable when Blakely pursued other women.

In April 1955, he left her and moved to Hampstead. On Good Friday, Ellis followed him, suspecting him of being with another woman. The following day, she drank a bottle of Pernod and waited for him outside the Magdala pub on South Hill Park, NW3. When Blakely emerged with a glass of beer, she shot him five times, the bullets killing him instantly.

During her trial she refused to plead manslaughter and when sentenced to death, refused any appeal.

Her execution led directly to the suspension of the death penalty ten years later.

5| 79 Gloucester Road SW7

This basement flat was leased by John Haigh, the acid-bath murderer, who was hanged on 10 August 1949. Here, he stored large quantities of petrol and acid.

Haigh's first victim was Donald McSwan, an ex-employer living in nearby Claverton Street. McSwan, who wanted to avoid military service, was lured to the basement by Haigh, knocked out and his remains dissolved in an acid-bath. In July 1945, to answer their questions, Haigh invited McSwan's parents to the flat and similarly killed them. He then procured McSwan's assets on which he lived for several years.

In February 1948, a similar fate fell upon Dr and Mrs Henderson after which Haigh forged papers to claim their estate. They were killed at his warehouse in Crawley, Sussex and Haigh returned to the Onslow Court Hotel, Queen's Gate, where he now lived.

The murder of his next victim, Mrs Durand-Deacon, a fellow resident at Onslow Court, was his undoing.

After shooting her at Crawley, he disposed of the body in the same way. However friends queried her absence and suspicion fell on Haigh as the last person to have seen her alive. Though evidence was found that he was selling off her jewellery, he was only arrested when remains of her body were found at the warehouse.

6| Iranian Embassy 16 Prince's Gate SW7

The upheaval of the Iranian Revolution the previous year came to South Kensington on 30 April 1980. The staff of the embassy and some foreign journalists were held hostage in the building by six separatists from Khuzistan wanting independence from Iran.

The SAS stormed the embassy after the body of a press officer had been thrown outside the door. They descended on ropes through windows and within seventeen minutes their spectacular raid was over. Five terrorists and one hostage were killed.

7| Pembridge Gardens W2

This was the scene of the first murder by Neville Heath, the notorious 'Lady Killer'.

Heath appeared a gentleman and indeed introduced himself as being a Colonel. But his civilised exterior masked his sadistic impulses. This was confirmed, when on 21 June 1946, at the Pembridge Court Hotel, the body of Margery Gardner, a woman known for her masochistic tendencies, was found with her genitals violently lacerated by human teeth.

The alarm was raised the following night by another girl whom Heath had brought to the hotel. But Heath had disappeared. The police traced him to a hotel in Bournemouth on 6 July, where he was staying under an assumed name. Unfortunately before their arrival, he had killed another woman, Doreen Marshall, in the same violent manner. He was executed at Pentonville prison.

8 | Plumber's Arms 14 Lower Belgrave Street SW1

On the morning of 7 November 1974, the Earl of Lucan began his usual day of privileged leisure. Friends with some of the richest people in the country, he spent his time gambling and entertaining at private Mayfair clubs. His only inconvenience was the messy separation from his wife.

By nightfall, it had all gone horribly wrong. His estranged wife staggered into this pub across the road from 46 Lower Belgrave Street. She was hysterical with traces of blood on her face. She claimed that her husband had attacked her. On reaching the house, the police found the battered body of the children's nanny, Sandra Rivett, but no sign of the Earl. It was thought Rivett had been mistaken for the Countess. An arrest warrant was issued and a nation-wide hunt ensued. But apart from Lucan's abandoned car at Newhaven, no trace of the Earl has ever been found. The case remains open.

9 | 18 St Leonard's Terrace SW3

This elegant Chelsea house was home to Bram Stoker, the creator of *Dracula*, the most famous vampire story ever written.

"As the Count leaned over me and his hands touched me, I could not repress a shudder. It may have been that his breath was rank, but a horrible feeling of nausea came over me, which do what I would, I could not conceal. … As if from down below in the valley, I heard the howling of many wolves. The Count's eyes gleamed and he said, 'Listen to them, the children of the night, what music they make'."

Count Dracula comes to England where he seeks victims, amongst them Lucy Westenra. She joins him as an un-dead and whilst by day she lies in Hampstead Cemetery, by night she prowls the area for human blood.

Stoker died in London in 1912 and was cremated, not buried, at Golders Green Cemetery.

JACK THE RIPPER NEWS OF HIS BRUTAL MURDERS HORRIFIED LONDON, AS REPORTED IN THE ILLUSTRATED POLICE NEWS

THE ILLUSTRATED POLICE NEWS
LAW COURTS AND WEEKLY RECORD

No. 1,292.   SATURDAY, NOVEMBER 17, 1888.   Price One Penny.

SKETCHES OF THE SEVENTH EAST END CRIME.

PHOTOGRAPHING THE BODY. — REMOVING THE BODY TO SHOREDITCH MORTUARY. — A MYSTERIOUS MAN WITH A BLACK BAG. — FORCING OPEN THE DOOR.

THE SEVENTH HORRIBLE MURDER BY THE MONSTER OF THE EAST-END.

MILLER'S COURT. MURDERER'S CHOSEN SPOT.

WINDOWS BOARDED UP.

THE SCENE OF THE MURDER, MILLER'S COURT.

THE SEVENTH VICTIM! PICKED OUT FOR SLAUGHTER BY THE EAST-END FIEND. FROM DESCRIPTIONS GIVEN BY HER INTIMATE FRIENDS.

THE AWFUL DISCOVERY BY McCARTHY.

STRANGE STORY TOLD OF A MAN WITH BLACK BAG.

THE MURDERER ESCAPING FROM THE WINDOW.

ARRESTED ON SUSPICION.

LOCALITY OF THE SEVEN UNDISCOVERED MURDERS.

REMOVING THE BODY.

ILLUSTRATED POLICE NEWS OFFERS £100 REWARD FOR THE CAPTURE OF THE WHITECHAPEL MURDERER.

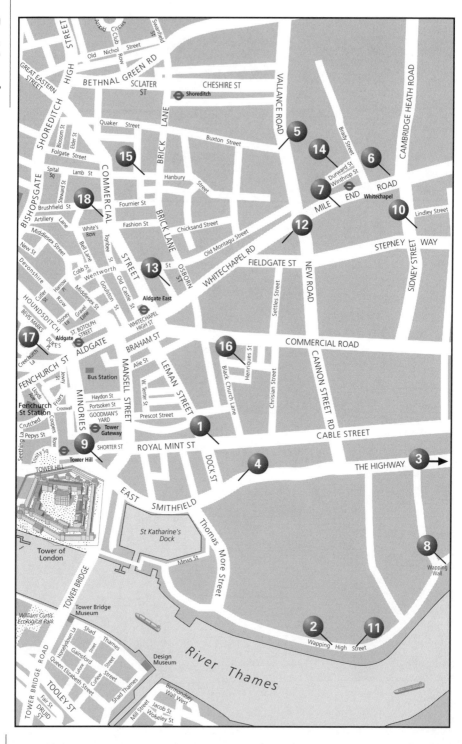

East London

London's wealth is based on trade and as the docks spread along the Thames so did crime. The cargoes that the ships brought were just too tempting for those living in the neighbouring communities.

All along the river narrow streets would be filled with pirates, prostitutes and drunken sailors. Violence was frequent as were executions.

Only after the Second World War did the docks begin their decline and with that the old ways of crime.

But by then other groups had formed and new methods found. Gangs like the Krays began to spread throughout the capital's underworld from the same tightly-bonded streets.

A century before the Kray twins ruled the area, around the dark alleys of Whitechapel, another sort of crime is famous. Jack the Ripper is England's most terrifying murderer, all the more frightening as he was never seen, never caught and known only through the butchery of his victims.

1│ Cable Street E1

On Sunday 4 October 1936, three hundred thousand protesters barricaded the Royal Mint Street end of Cable Street against the march of Sir Oswald Mosley's fascist Blackshirts through the East end of London. Fighting broke out when left-wing groups aided the local residents in blocking the march's route at Cable Street. In the ensuing violence, Mosley was forced to call off the march.

However the following week the fascists returned to the area, shouting anti-Jewish slogans and destroying the many Jewish shops along the Mile End Road.

The Cable Street Riots marked the frightening high point of British Fascism, just before the outbreak of the Second World War and modelled closely on the German Nazis.

2│ Execution Dock Wapping High Street E1

Between the fifteenth and nineteenth centuries, punishment for piracy was

EXECUTION DOCK
THE HANGMAN'S NOOSE
STANDS IN FRONT OF THE
PROSPECT OF WHITBY PUB

FROM THE EARLY EIGHTEENTH CENTURY, THE POPULATION OF ENGLAND BEGAN TO GROW. FUELLED BY THE INDUSTRIAL REVOLUTION AND THE MOVE TOWARDS CITIES, PEOPLE BECAME MORE TRANSIENT AND CONSEQUENTLY CRIME INCREASED. THE AUTHORITIES HAD TO FIND A WAY OF ERADICATING BRITAIN OF THIS 'CRIMINAL ELEMENT' AND TRANSPORTATION WAS THE ANSWER.

CONVICTS BEGAN TO BE TRANSPORTED TO BRITAIN'S COLONIES, MOSTLY TO THE EASTERN COAST OF THE PRESENT UNITED STATES OF AMERICA. FIFTY THOUSAND WERE TRANSPORTED TO AMERICA BEFORE THE AMERICAN WAR OF INDEPENDENCE IN 1776 MADE THIS IMPOSSIBLE. THE AUTHORITIES WERE FORCED TO LOOK ELSEWHERE.

THE SOLUTION WAS FOUND ON THE OTHER SIDE OF THE WORLD WITH THE OTHERWISE USELESS LANDS OF AUSTRALIA. BY 1867, UP TO TWO HUNDRED THOUSAND HAD BEEN SENT TO COLONISE THE AREA.

execution. During the growth of London's docks, piracy had become a massive problem with cargoes frequently damaged and plundered by organised gangs. Indeed, so bad did the problem become, that in addition to the deterrence of execution, the River Police were established in 1789.

Between Wapping New Stairs and King Henry's Stairs at low tide can still be seen the spot where those condemned of piracy were hanged for thirty minutes and then chained to a stake for three high tides to submerge them. Execution here was known as 'receiving the grace of Wapping'.

In 1701, the famous pirate Captain Kidd was executed at Wapping. Kidd had been a naval captain who turned to piracy after his murder of a sailor had made him an outlaw. As he lay chained on the shore, he looked at the large crowd gathered and saw an ex-lover laughing. "I have lain with that bitch three times, " he lamented, "and now she's come to see me hanged."

3│ Gill Street E14
off map: nearest station Westferry DLR

Here in 1913, whilst investigating the opium trade in the heart of China Town around The Causeway, the hack journalist Arthur Ward was inspired to create the master criminal Fu Manchu after seeing a Chinaman enter a car. Ward described the man as being "part of the most ghastly menace to our civilisation since Attila the Hun. His face the living appearance of evil."

Using the pseudonym Sax Rohmer, Ward went on to write thirteen books featuring Fu Manchu and based in this area.

4│ The Highway E1

This busy road encompasses the notorious Ratcliffe Highway. It was infamous as an area controlled by gangs involved in all forms of vice who preyed particularly on the visiting sailors.

In December 1811, seven murders took place here which horrified the nation and led to demands, not heard since the 1780 Gordon Riots, for the setting up of a professional police force.

At midnight on 7 December, a draper, his family and an apprentice were murdered at their home at 29 The Highway. The murder weapons, a gore-covered chisel and heavy wooden hammer, were found at the scene.

Days later, the bodies of the nearby King's Arms Tavern publican, his wife and maid were found. Their throats had been cut to the spine.

Terror spread throughout the nation. The local watchmen were ill-equipped and unable to come up with any clues and after forty false arrests which did nothing to appease public opinion, all were sacked.

Only when a sailor, John Williams, hanged himself after his arrest did people believe that the killer had been found. Williams was buried, with the murder weapons and a stake through his heart, at the corner of Cable Street and Cannon Street Road.

Vallance Road home to London's notorious gangsters of the 1960s, the Kray Twins

THE BLIND BEGGAR
SCENE OF THE INFAMOUS KRAY
GANGLAND MURDER

The Krays
5 | Vallance Road E1
During the 1960s the dominant criminal gang in London was that controlled by the twins, Ronnie and Reggie Kray.

They had grown up during the Second World War in the tight-knit community around their home in Vallance Road. After periods in reform school and jail, they built an empire based on extortion, prostitution and gambling. Modelling themselves on the American Mafia, they infiltrated the legitimate world via casinos and west-end night-clubs.

Though they used extreme violence to maintain their authority, the Krays cultivated an aura of pop-star sophistication and surrounded themselves with celebrities.

For a period in the early sixties, the police were powerless to exert any control over their activities. None of the charges brought against the twins could stick in court. Indeed it was thought subsequently that much of their protection came from their links with the Establishment. For example, Ronnie, a homosexual, supplied boys to the bisexual Lord Boothby, a cabinet minister and lover of Dorothy Macmillan, wife of the Prime Minister.

6 | The Blind Beggar 337 Whitechapel Road E1
Their downfall began as Ronnie's mental instability led him to more and greater acts of extreme violence. On 8 March 1966 he entered the Blind Beggar pub and, in front of customers, shot dead George Cornell, a member of the rival Richardson gang from South London. Soon afterwards, a second victim, Jack McVitie, was killed in Stoke Newington.

Though it was commonly known that the Krays were responsible for the deaths, the police investigations led nowhere. A wall of terrified silence surrounded the twins. No eye witnesses would speak and no-one would come forward with any information. Only after eight months, with a team of twenty-seven men, did the police feel confident enough to arrest the twins. Once in custody witnesses began to emerge. The Kray's fate was sealed. At the end of a long trial at the Old Bailey in 1968, the two brothers were each sentenced to a minimum of thirty years in jail.

Ronnie Kray died at Broadmoor Hospital for the criminally insane in March 1995. But so great had the myth of the Krays grown, that the streets of the East End came to a virtual standstill as his funeral cortege passed through.

7 | **London Hospital** Whitechapel Road E1

Founded in 1740 and moved to Whitechapel in 1757, the hospital became home to Joseph Merrick who lived in a flat under the roof. Known as the Elephant Man because of the gross skin and bone deformities of his skull and arm, Merrick was brought up in workhouses from infancy until the age of seventeen when he worked in freak shows. In 1886, he was rescued from his life of torment by the surgeon Frederick Treves and brought to the hospital to live.

During his four years at the hospital he became a society celebrity, visited by the famous and royalty. He died on 11 April 1890 at the age of twenty-eight when he attempted to sleep on his back, a position that he had always wanted to try because it was 'normal'. However the weight of his vast skull was too much and it bent back during sleep, breaking his neck. His skeleton is kept at the hospital.

8 | **The Prospect of Whitby** 57 Wapping Wall E1

This historic riverside pub was originally built in 1520 when surrounded by empty fields. It was first known as the Devil's Tavern and soon became a haunt for smugglers and thieves, who sold bodies dragged from the Thames to medical schools.

Later the pub was frequented by Judge Jeffries, who lived in nearby Butcher Row and would often come here to watch the men he had condemned to death hang at Wapping's Execution dock.

In 1777, in an effort to improve its image, the pub changed its name to that of a locally moored ship, which transported coal to London from Newcastle. And in 1780, the first fuschia was sold here by a sailor, recently returned from the West Indies, for a quarter pint of rum.

Dickens, Whistler and Turner were regulars at the pub in the nineteenth century, as was Gustave Dore who drew pictures of London lowlife here.

9 | **Royal Mint** East Smithfield E1

In the fourteenth century, this was the site of a plague pit, consecrated by Bishop Stratford in 1349 and containing hundreds of victims of the Black Death.

It was excavated during the construction of the present building. The plague pits were found to be full of skeletons. One pit was over 70 metres wide by 130 metres long.

PLAGUES

PLAGUES HAVE TERRORISED AND RAVAGED LONDON'S POPULATION FOR THE LAST THOUSAND YEARS. THE FIRST RECORDED PLAGUE WAS IN AD 664 WHICH SEVERELY DEPOPULATED THE SOUTH OF ENGLAND. EPIDEMICS WERE FREQUENT

THE DISEASE WAS CARRIED BY FLEAS NESTLING IN THE FUR OF RATS. HOWEVER IGNORANCE OF ITS CAUSE AND LACK OF SANITATION RESULTED IN THE POPULATION HAVING NO PROTECTION. INDEED DURING THE GREAT PLAGUE OF THE SEVENTEENTH CENTURY, THE ONLY PREDATOR OF THE RAT, DOMESTIC DOGS AND CATS, WERE THEMSELVES THOUGHT RESPONSIBLE. WITHIN DAYS OF THE OUTBREAK, FORTY THOUSAND DOGS AND TWO HUNDRED THOUSAND CATS WERE SLAUGHTERED ALLOWING THE RATS TO LIVE UNCHECKED SO THAT ONLY IN THE FREEZING WINTER MONTHS DID THE PLAGUE ABATE.

THE BUBONIC PLAGUE, DURING 1348-9, WAS NOT THE FIRST, BUT IT WAS ESPECIALLY DEVASTATING, CLAIMING UP TO HALF THE POPULATION OF LONDON. THE GREAT PLAGUE OF 1664 CLAIMED OVER A HUNDRED THOUSAND LIVES IN EIGHTEEN MONTHS. WHEREVER THE PLAGUE CAME, PANIC SPREAD. SUFFERERS WERE SEALED IN THEIR HOUSES. THOSE THAT COULD, FLED LONDON AS PUBLIC ORDER BROKE DOWN.

10 | Sidney Street Siege E1

In December 1910, a group of anti-Tsarist terrorists were cornered by police in a jewellery shop at 119 Houndsditch, after an attempted robbery. However they escaped, killing three policemen. The massive outcry prompted a country-wide search.

But on 3 January 1911, they were traced to 100 Sidney Street. The terrorists had barricaded themselves into the property keeping the authorities at bay with gun-shot for five hours. Included in the crowd outside was Winston Churchill, then Home Secretary, who had come to view the scene. The siege only ended when the terrorists set light to the house, dying in the flames.

11 | Town of Ramsgate 62 Wapping High Street E1

This riverside pub, with a balcony overlooking the Thames, was originally known as the Red Cow, reputedly after a bad-tempered red-haired barmaid; the present name derives from the Kent fishermen who landed their fish next door at Wapping Old Stairs. From the balcony at low tide, you can see the posts at which pirates were executed at Execution Dock.

In 1688 the notorious Judge Jeffries, responsible for hundreds of executions, was arrested at the pub whilst trying to escape England, after his fall from power with the exile of King James II.

During the eighteenth century, the cellars of the pub were used as dungeons for convicts awaiting transportation to America and Australia.

12 | 130 Whitechapel Road E1

In September 1874, at a warehouse which stood behind the factory standing here today, Henry Wainwright carried out a gruesome murder.

Wainwright was a respectable businessman with a wife and four children living in a nearby prosperous square. He successfully hid the presence of his mistress, Harriet Lane, and their two daughters, from his family and managed to keep the two lives going until he hit upon hard times. His mistress was the one to suffer, financially, and she began to complain. Wainwright decided to end the affair and when her continued complaints annoyed him further, he planned her murder. Harriet came to this warehouse to meet with Wainwright and this was where he shot her dead. After her throat had been cut, he buried her. No-one was suspicious.

However, when the lease on the warehouse expired the next year, Wainwright panicked and decided to move the body to his brother's premises in Borough. Harriet's body was packaged into several parcels and, with the help of an unknowing ex-employee, Stokes, he called a cab to transport them to London Bridge. Stokes was curious as to what was in these odd-shaped and probably odorous parcels and he saw one of Harriet's hands. Yet he still helped Wainwright into the cab.

The cab drove through the City and Stokes ran after the vehicle, calling all the time for a policeman. Wainwright was finally arrested at the south London warehouse with the parcels in his hands.

Wainwright was hanged at Newgate on 21 December 1875 after a trial that attracted much attention. The Lord Mayor of London invited over eighty people to watch the notorious murderer hang.

Jack the Ripper: The Whitechapel Murders E1

Only a few streets remain unchanged from this area of late-nineteenth century slums. And nothing remains of the atmosphere of terror and panic that gripped these streets, and indeed all of London, during the three hot months of late summer in 1888 when 'the Ripper' murders froze the population in fear.

Jack the Ripper is the name given to the perpetrator of some of the most mysterious and grizzly murders. Few clues were left, other than the bodies, each skillfully mutilated and disembowelled. Some claimed the murderer to be a prostitute-hater, others that he was a madman. At various times suspects have come under the spotlight but none conclusively.

There was even the rumour that the murderer was the surgeon of the Royal family. The theory is based on Mary Kelly, the last victim, being a midwife and witness to the illegitimate birth of a child by the Queen's grandson, the Duke of Clarence. If this were true, the previous five women would have either been killed mistakenly or to disguise the fact that Mary Kelly was the intended victim. Whatever the reasons for the murders, no more were committed after her death.

The police investigations of the murders were massive in response to public fears. However nobody was ever charged and whoever Jack the Ripper was, he disappeared in November 1888 as mysteriously as he had arrived.

13 | Gunthorpe Street

Martha Turner was the first to die, on 7 August 1888, discovered dead on the first floor of George Yard Buildings, off Whitechapel Road.

14 | Durward Street

Mary Ann Nicholls was found on 31 August 1888 on the pavement. After her husband had left her, she had turned to prostitution and had just left a Brick Lane pub to look for a customer when she was killed.

15 | 29 Hanbury Street

Annie Chapman, the wife of a vet, who had become an alcoholic and a prostitute, was found on 8 September in the backyard of this house.

16 | 40 Henriques Street

The body of Elizabeth Stride was found on 30 September behind a working man's club. Her husband and children had recently drowned when the pleasure steamer, the Princess Alice, had sunk in the Thames.

17 | Mitre Square EC3

Catherine Eddowes' murdered corpse was found in this dark square on 30 September.

18 | White's Row & Brushfield Street

Mary Kelly was discovered on 9 November inside her own home at 13 Miller's Court, now a car park. Her body was the most brutally disfigured. She was also, unaccountably, the last victim.

AND THE GREAT FIRE OF LONDON IN 1666, THOUGH DESTROYING MUCH OF THE CITY, AT LEAST FUMIGATED WHAT WAS LEFT, ESPECIALLY AS THE REBUILDING WAS CARRIED OUT IN STONE.

THE PLAGUE MOVED FROM INFECTION TO DEATH VERY SWIFTLY. A HEALTHY PERSON WOULD HAVE NO MORE THAN A COUPLE OF DAYS FROM SEEING THE FIRST SIGN OF RED CIRCLES ON HIS SKIN, FOLLOWED BY HIS BREATH BECOMING PUTRID, HIS LUNGS BECOMING BLOCKED AND HIS CONTINUAL SNEEZING, TO HIS DEATH.

OF THE MANY SONGS WRITTEN ABOUT THE GREAT PLAGUE PERHAPS THE MOST EVOCATIVE IS THE CHILDREN'S NURSERY RHYME STILL SUNG IN SCHOOL PLAYGROUNDS:

"RING A RING A ROSES
A POCKET FULL OF POSES
A TISSUE, A TISSUE
WE ALL FALL DOWN"

MURDERED PLAYWRIGHT JOE ORTON RELAXING IN HIS ROOM AT 25 NOEL ROAD

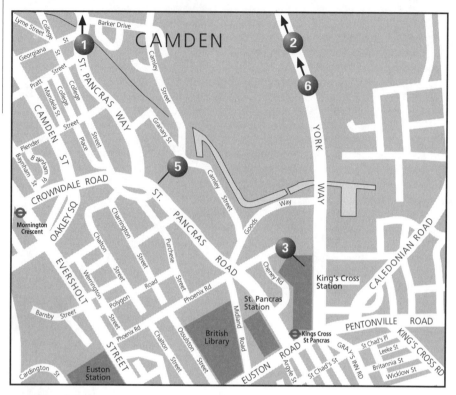

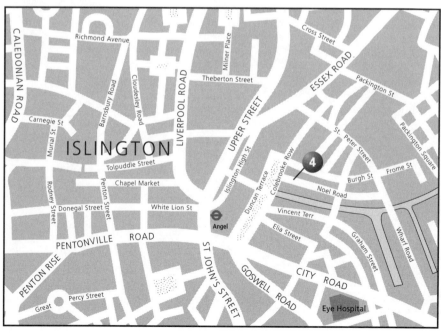

CRANLEY GARDENS
HOME TO SERIAL KILLER DENNIS
NILSEN

North London

North London is a series of villages built on hills. The romantic tree-lined streets and distant views have made attractive homes for centuries.

But there is another side to North London. Small flats and bedsits house lonely and alienated people living anonymous lives of unsuspected desperation. For Dennis Nilsen, this exploded into serial murder. Others, like Dr. Crippen and the lover of Joe Orton, simply wanted a release from unhappy love.

1│ 23 Cranley Gardens Muswell Hill N10
off map: nearest tube Highgate
Some of the most macabre murders ever to have taken place occurred in the attic flat of this suburban house.

Dennis Nilsen moved here aged thirty-seven in 1981. He was a nondescript civil servant who worked at the Kentish Town Job Centre. Previously, he had spent eleven years in the army and some time in the police force. Without friends and a repressed homosexual, he later described himself as "living in total social isolation and in a desperate search for a sexual identity."

His victims were all male, mostly drifters and fellow lost souls he met in pubs in the area. Nilsen would ask them back to Cranley Gardens where he would kill them. The bodies remained in the flat until putrefication. Nilsen claimed this was so as to retain some friendship.

When they decomposed, he dismembered them for disposal, some parts down the drain, some buried in the garden and some dumped in rubbish bins. He was arrested after complaints of blocked drains from other tenants in the building revealed the crimes.

Nilsen was charged with murdering three men. However, it is thought that he in fact murdered fifteen or sixteen men in total, several at a former residence, 195 Melrose Avenue, Cricklewood. It is possible he murdered more as by virtue of the type of victim he chose, there were few people to notice their disappearance.

Nilsen is serving a life sentence at Broadmoor Hospital.

2 | 39 Hilldrop Crescent N7

off map: nearest tube Holloway Road

Just around the corner from Holloway Prison and close to Pentonville, stood the home of Dr Hawley Harvey Crippen.

In July 1910, the body of his second wife, Cora, was discovered in what is now Margaret Bondfield House. Her head was never found. She had been killed, probably in January 1910, with the poison hyoscin hydrobromide. His first wife had also died suspiciously.

Crippen fled by ship to Canada on 20 July 1910, disguising his lover, Ethel le Neve, as his son. The captain became suspicious of the relationship, having read of the murder in London and the hunt for Crippen. Using the newly installed telegraph, his suspicions were confirmed and as Crippen disembarked, he was arrested by British police who had taken a faster boat from Liverpool.

Crippen hanged at Pentonville Prison on 23 November 1910.

3 | King's Cross Station N1

A tragic disaster of recent years occurred here on 19 November 1987. Thirty people died and many suffered appalling burns after a fire swept through the underground station. Caused by an electrical fault on a wooden escalator, the fire raged unchecked when the sprinkler system failed to work.

NOEL ROAD
HOME OF JOE ORTON AND HIS
MURDERER KENNETH HALLIWELL

4| 25 Noel Road N1

On 9 August 1967, the playwright Joe Orton was beaten to death with a hammer by his lover of sixteen years, Kenneth Halliwell. The murder took place at 25 Noel Road, their home together since 1959.

Orton was at the height of his success having written the comedies *Entertaining Mr Sloane* and *What the Butler Saw*. However, his promiscuity had caused Halliwell to become fatally jealous.

Halliwell took an overdose of pills straight after fatally hammering Orton with nine blows to his head. Ironically, it was Halliwell who died first.

5| St Pancras Old Church Pancras Road NW1

This ancient church has several connections to the criminal world of London.

● Jonathan Wild (**see p.52**), the most important criminal of eighteenth century London, was married in the church in 1718. After his execution, he was buried here in 1725. However his body did not rest in peace as two days later it was dug up and placed in a gibbet. After the flesh had withered away, his skeleton was taken to the Royal College of Surgeons for display.

● The incorrigible thief, Jenny Diver (real name Mary Young) was buried here after being hanged on 18 March 1740. She was executed after several attempts to transport her had failed. Each time she had returned from America to London and reverted to her old ways of stealing for a living.

6| 14 Waterlow Road (once Bismarck Road) N19

off map: nearest tube Archway

This was the last home of George Joseph Smith, the infamous 'Brides in the Bath Murderer'. Smith had drowned three wives to claim insurance money and was hanged on 13 August 1915.

Bessie Mundy died on 13 July 1912 at Herne Bay in a zinc bath which he had recently purchased. The following day he returned the bath to the shop, claiming he no longer needed it. The next wife to die was Alice Burnham, who similarly drowned in the bath on 12 December 1913 in Blackpool, four weeks after their marriage.

Margaret Lofty died here, again in the bath, at 14 Waterlow Road on 18 December 1914, the day after her marriage to Smith. Margaret had just that morning written a will leaving everything she had to her new husband and had emptied the savings out of her post office account.

It was the relatives of Alice Burnham who alerted the police to their suspicions about Smith when they read of Margaret's murder in the papers.

LONDON BURNING DURING THE BLITZ THE AFTERMATH OF GERMAN BOMBING

Appendix

MUSEUMS OF INTEREST

Britain At War Experience 64-66 Tooley Street SE1
Tel. 0171-403 3171
Open Apr-Sept: daily 10am-5.30pm
     Oct-Mar: daily 10am-4.30pm
Admission charge
Nearest tube London Bridge
Excellent recreation of life in London during the Blitz.

Cabinet War Rooms Clive Steps, King Charles Street SW1
Tel. 0171-930 6961
Open daily 10am-6pm
Admission charge
Nearest tube Westminster
Underground offices where Churchill's men controlled and plotted the movements of the Allied Army during the Second World War.

Clink Prison 1 Clink Street SE1
Tel. 0171-378 1558
Open daily 10am-6pm
Admission charge
Nearest tube London Bridge
Museum displaying life in prison from medieval times, with exhibits on punishment and torture.
(see p.48)

House of Detention Clerkenwell Close EC1
Tel. 0171-253 9494
Open daily 10am-6pm
Admission charge
Nearest tube Farringdon
Atmospheric prison museum housed in the original underground cells.
(see p.32)

Imperial War Museum Lambeth Road SE1
Tel. 0171-416 5000
Open daily 10am-6pm
Admission charge
Nearest tube Lambeth North
The museum has a vast range of displays relating to the two World Wars and other conflicts involving Britain this century. The exhibition about the Blitz, London's direct experience of the Second World War, is very informative.
(see p.49)

London Dungeons 28-34 Tooley Street SE1
Tel. 0171-403 0606
Open Apr-Sept: daily 10am-6.30pm
Oct-Mar: daily 10am-5.30pm
Admission charge
Nearest tube London Bridge
A series of tableaux show scenes of torture, plague and prison from
Medieval times.

Madame Tussaud's Waxworks Marylebone Road NW1
Tel. 0171-935 6861
Open daily 9am-5.30pm (winter: Mon-Fri 10am-5.30pm & w/e 9.30am-
5.30pm)
Admission charge
Nearest tube Baker Street
After making death masks of victims of the guillotine, Mme Tussaud came
to London to set up her own waxworks in 1835. The Chamber of Horrors
graphically illustrates characters from London's grizzly past.

Museum of London 150 London Wall EC2
Tel. 0171-600 3699
Open Tues-Sat 10am-5.50pm & Sun 12-5.50pm
Admission charge
Nearest tube Barbican/St Paul's/Moorgate
This comprehensive museum of the history of London has excellent displays
on the plagues, prisons, Bethlehem Royal Hospital and the Great Fire of
London.

Old Operating Theatre Museum St Thomas's Street SE1
Tel. 0171-955 4791
Open daily 10am-4pm (closed some Mondays)
Admission charge
Nearest tube London Bridge
Restored to its original form, the operating theatre houses exhibitions of
surgery in pre-modern times, before anaesthetics and antiseptics.

Wellcome Museum of the History of Medicine Science Museum,
Exhibition Road SW7
Tel. 0171-938 8008
Open daily 10am-6pm (Sun 11am-8pm)
Admission charge
Nearest tube South Kensington
On the top floor of the Science Museum, these galleries display the story of
medicine from pre-history to the present. The horrors of early medicine are
clearly revealed.

Index